USN PHANTOMS in combat

by Lou Drendel

illustrated by Lou Drendel

squadron/signal publications

An F-4J Phantom of VF-96 overflies the USS CONSTELLATION (CVA-64) during cyclic operations in the South China Sea, as an RA-5C Vigilante is launched off the port bow catapult.

ISBN 0-89747-213-6

If you have any photographs of the aircraft, armor, soldiers or ships of any nation, particularly wartime snapshots, why not share them with us and help make Squadron/Signal's books all the more interesting and complete in the future. Any photograph sent to us will be copied and the original returned. The donor will be fully credited for any photos used. Please send them to:

Squadron/Signal Publications, Inc.
1115 Crowley Drive.
Carrollton, TX 75011-5010.

Photo Credits

U.S. Navy
McDonnell Douglas
Tailhook Photo Service
Norman E. Taylor
Burner Beardsley
Jim Hurley
R. J. Archer
RADM James H. Flatley III
Nicholas J. Waters III
Gene Tucker
Robert J Lawson
Shinichi Ohtaki
Jim Sullivan

INTRODUCTION

The McDonnell Douglas F-4 Phantom II is in its 30th year of operational service as this book goes to press. That is a remarkable accomplishment for any aircraft and is usually reserved for more staid types, such as the Douglas DC-3. For a front-line fighter to serve that long, where combat is fast, furious, and survivable only by those at the leading edge of technology, is even more astounding. The McDonnell Aircraft engineers designed an aircraft in the late 1950s which surmounted an aerodynamic design plateau which has endured to this day (with only minor modifications). This book is not a 'nuts and bolts' design history of the Phantom, but since the Phantom II was originally designed for the Navy, it seems appropriate to include a brief pictorial design history in 'U.S. Navy Phantoms in Combat'.

Ironically, the most prolific fighter of modern times began life as a loser. The fledgling Phantom II came in second to the Vought F8U Crusader in the Navy design competition to acquire its first supersonic fighter. The Crusader was a prototypical fighter; single seat, single engine, armed with guns, and having no fire-control radar. It was a fighter pilot's dream...a pure VFR supersonic dogfighting machine, designed for one-on-one combat in the supersonic age. The losing McDonnell entry had also been a single-seater with a gun, but it came at the dawn of the age of the missileers...the proponents of the missile armed interceptor. Their reasoning went something like this; "Why get in close and grunt under heavy G while you went round and round with the enemy, when it was much easier to blast him out of the sky from long range with a sophisticated air-to-air missile?" As a result, the follow-on McDonnell fighter design diverged radically from accepted fighter aircraft design criteria of the day. In addition to being twin engined, the AH-1, as it was then known, had a second cockpit, no guns, and a sophisticated fire control system to fire the new, long range Sparrow Air-to-Air Missiles (AAMs). The original engines were J-65s, but they were soon replaced by the new, more powerful J-79. This engine would make the Phantom II the Navy's first fighter capable of reaching Mach 2.

The Phantom II emerged from the McDonnell factory at St. Louis with a new Navy designation, F4H-1. McDonnell test pilot R.C. Little made the first flight on 27 May 1958. Ike was in the White House, rock and roll was only three years old, gasoline was less than 30 cents a gallon, television was black and white, and every adult in America had vivid memories of World War II. That same year the Phantom II was pitted against the follow-on version of the Crusader in a competition to select the Navy's next generation fleet fighter. Vought had produced a refinement of their excellent Crusader fighter, the F8U-3, while McDonnell had designed a pure fleet defense interceptor, the F4H-1. The Navy wanted the Phantom II's all-weather long-range intercept capability and they announced the Phantom II as the winner on 17 December 1958. The fledgling Phantom II was six years away from its baptism of fire. During that intervening six years, the Phantom II would undergo a number of design changes, break every major speed and time to climb altitude record, and be adopted by every American service as its primary fighter. Navy Phantoms did all of the preliminary testing and record-setting flights. Navy Phantoms were also the first to see combat in Southeast Asia, flying Barrier Combat Air Patrol (BARCAP) missions for the retributive strikes launched by USS TICONDEROGA and USS CONSTELLATION that followed the Tonkin Gulf Incident of 2 August 1964. When the Naval air war began in earnest on 7 February 1966, Phantom squadrons were in the forefront, where they remained until the American pull-out from Southeast Asia some seven years later.

The sixth production F4H-1 Phantom II (BuNo 143391) is positioned on the TC7 land-based steam catapult, during carrier suitability tests held in January of 1960. The Phantom has been fitted with a instrumented nose probe mounted on the tip of the radome. (U.S. Navy)

(Above) The Phantom underwent shipboard carrier suitability testing aboard USS FRANKLIN D. ROOSEVELT (CVA-42) during December of 1961. The early Phantom had a faired upper intake lip which was later removed because it caused problems with airflow separation. (U.S. Navy)

(Above) Plane handlers prepare to start the sixth production Phantom during carrier deck trials on 5 June 1961. The planked deck indicates that this is one of the small deck carriers, believed to be USS INTREPID, which hosted trials in April of 1960. (U.S. Navy)

(Above) Deck crews position an early F4H-1 on the number one catapult of USS INDEPENDENCE (CVA-62) during carrier suitability trials held in February of 1960. (U.S. Navy)

(Below) The first Phantom (BuNo 142259) was to be used for an altitude record attempt by McDonnell test pilot Gerald Huelsbeck. On 21 October 1959, during a test flight leading up to the record attempt, the right rear engine access door separated, disrupting engine cooling and causing an engine fire. The aircraft crashed, killing Huelsbeck. (McDonnell Aircraft)

CDR D.D. Engen climbs aboard an early F4H-1 Phantom II. Engen would later head the Federal Aviation Administration (FAA) upon his retirement from the Navy. The nose radome contained special instruments for measuring aircraft performance during testing. (U.S. Navy)

(Above) President Dwight D. Eisenhower looked the Phantom over for the first time at NAS North Island, San Diego, California on 21 October 1960. Within ninety days he would make his famous parting speech, warning of the dangers of the "Military Industrial Complex." (U.S. Navy)

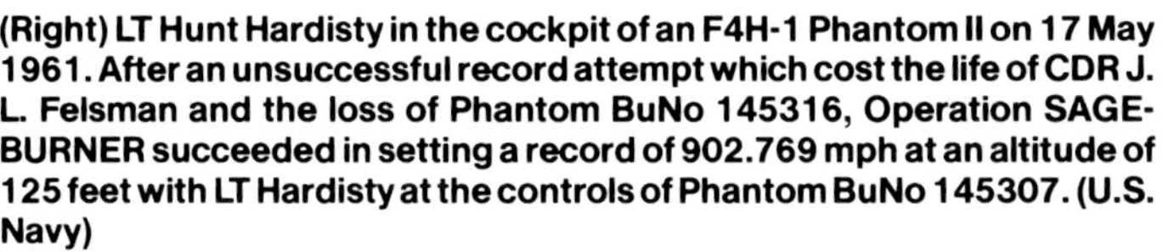
(Right) LT Hunt Hardisty in the cockpit of an F4H-1 Phantom II on 17 May 1961. After an unsuccessful record attempt which cost the life of CDR J. L. Felsman and the loss of Phantom BuNo 145316, Operation SAGEBURNER succeeded in setting a record of 902.769 mph at an altitude of 125 feet with LT Hardisty at the controls of Phantom BuNo 145307. (U.S. Navy)

(Below) An F-4B Phantom II of the service test unit at the Naval Air Test Center, Patuxent River, Maryland, tests an early model Buddy store air-to-air refueling pod on 12 November 1964. (U.S. Navy)

(Above) Catapult crews position *GOLDEN NUGGET* on the shore based steam catapult at NAS Lakehurst, New Jersey on 8 March 1963. The F-4B uses full extension of the nose gear strut in order to achieve a higher angle of attack for launch. (U.S. Navy)

(Left) The first Phantom fatality resulted from an unsuccessful low altitude, high-speed ejection (McDonnell test pilot Huelsbeck). This accident resulted in renewed testing, including mounting the forward fuselage of an F-4B on a rocket test sled at NAS China Lake to test a 600 mph ejection seat on 12 December 1968. (U.S. Navy)

A number of famous pilots were involved in testing, or operational use of the Phantom, including (left to right) future astronauts LT Charles 'Pete' Conrad, LCDR John W. Young, and CDR Bruce McCandless, (front) who flew F-4B Phantoms aboard the USS CORAL SEA (CVA-43) before being selected to the astronaut program. (U.S. Navy)

(Above) An F-4A Phantom of the flight test division at NAS Pax River comes aboard USS MIDWAY (CVA-41) during tests of the Automatic Carrier Landing System (ACLS) during June of 1965. The legend, *LOOK MA NO HANDS*, was carried on the fuselage side in Black. (U.S. Navy)

(Below) WO2 J. H. Gloce mans the front cockpit while LCDR K.W. Stecker straps into the rear cockpit of this VF-121 F-4B at NAS Miramar, California on 16 May 1961. VF-121 was the West Coast Replacement Air Group (RAG) responsible for training new Phantom pilots and RIOs for fleet squadrons. (U.S. Navy)

(Above) A flight of BeDevilers Phantoms prepare for launch from the port catapult aboard USS FORRESTAL (CVA-59) during March of 1963. VF-74 was the first operational East Coast Phantom II squadron, commanded by CDR Julian S. Lake. (U.S. Navy)

(Below) This F4H-1 (F-4A) of VF-101 Detachment A, carries Red fuselage stripes during *Project Lana*. *Project Lana* was conceived as part of the celebration of the 50th anniversary of Naval Aviation and used five F-4s to dash across the United States (from west to east) in two hours and forty-eight minutes on 24 May 1961. (McDonnell Aircraft)

THE PLAYERS

Combat for American F-4 Phantom II squadrons was limited to the war in Southeast Asia and during the war (1963 - 1975) a number of Navy fighter squadrons were involved. The following is a list of these squadrons along with the carrier they were deployed aboard for their combat cruises.

(Above) An F-4B of VF-41 Black Aces makes a go-around after boltering (missing the arresting gear) aboard USS INDEPENDENCE (CVA-62) on 20 June 1963. VF-41 was the third operational East Coast Phantom squadron, being declared operational during March of 1962. (U.S. Navy)

Squadron	Air Wing	Carrier	Date(s)
VF-11	CVW-17	FORRESTAL (CVA-59)	JUN 67 - JUL 73
VF-14	CVW-1	ROOSEVELT (CVA-42)	APR 64 - APR 68
VF-21	CVW-2	MIDWAY (CVA-41)	NOV 63 - NOV 65
		CORAL SEA (CVA-43)	JUL 66 - FEB 67
		RANGER (CVA-61)	NOV 67 - MAY 68
VF-31	CVW-3	SARATOGA (CVA-60)	NOV 64 - DEC 67
			JUL 69 - AUG 80
VF-32	CVW-1	ROOSEVELT (CVA-42)	JUN 66 - JUN 68
VF-33	CVW-6	AMERICA (CVA-66)	APR 68 - JAN 69
VF-41	CVW-7	INDEPENDENCE (CVA-62)	AUG 63 - FEB 67
VF-51	CVW-15	CORAL SEA (CVA-43)	NOV 71 - NOV 73
VF-74	CVW-17	FORRESTAL (CVA-59)	JUN 67
VF-84	CVW-7	INDEPENDENCE (CVA-62)	FEB 65 - FEB 67
VF-92	CVW-9	ENTERPRISE (CVAN-65)	OCT 65 - JUL 68
		CONSTELLATION (CVA-64)	OCT 71 - DEC 74
VF-96	CVW-9	ENTERPRISE (CVAN-65)	OCT 65 - JUL 68
		CONSTELLATION (CVA-64)	OCT 71 - DEC 74
VF-102	CVW-6	AMERICA (CVA-66)	APR 68 - JAN 69
VF-103	CVW-3	SARATOGA (CVA-60)	MAR 66 - DEC 67
			JUL 69 - AUG 80
VF-111	CVW-15	CORAL SEA (CVA-43)	NOV 71 - NOV 73
VF-114	CVW-11	KITTY HAWK (CVA-63)	SEP 62 - DEC 75
VF-142	CVW-14	CONSTELLATION (CVA-64)	MAY 64 - FEB 65
			APR 67 - MAY 70
		RANGER (CVA-60)	DEC 65 - AUG 66
		ENTERPRISE (CVAN-65)	JUN 71 - JUN 73
VF-143	CVW-14	CONSTELLATION (CVA-64)	FEB 63 - FEB 65
			APR 67 - MAY 70
		RANGER (CVA-61)	DEC 65 - AUG 66
		ENTERPRISE (CVAN-65)	JUN 71 - JUN 73
VF-151	CVW-15	CORAL SEA (CVA-43)	DEC 64 - NOV 65
			JUL 67 - JUL 70
		CONSTELLATION (CVA-64)	MAY 66 - DEC 66
		MIDWAY (CVA-41)	APR 71 - MAR 73
VF-154	CVW-2	CORAL SEA (CVA-43)	JUL 66 - FEB 67
		RANGER (CVA-60)	NOV 67 - MAY 68
VF-161	CVW-15	CONSTELLATION (CVA-64)	MAY 66 - DEC 66
		CORAL SEA (CVA-43)	JUL 67 - JUL 70
	CVW-5	MIDWAY (CVA-41)	APR 71 - MAR 73
VF-213	CVW-11	KITTY HAWK (CVA-63)	OCT 66 - DEC 75

(Below) A fully armed F-4B of VF-96 high over the Western Pacific during December of 1964. VF-96 was the second operational West Coast Phantom squadron deploying aboard USS RANGER (CVA-61) during 1964 and 1965. (U.S. Navy)

(Below) Armed with Sparrow and Sidewinder air-to-air missiles, this F-4B of VF-143 Puking Dogs was deployed to WESTPAC during July of 1963. VF-143, along with its sister squadron VF-142, were embarked aboard USS CONSTELLATION (CVA-64). (U.S. Navy)

Captain Gene Tucker

...is one of those people who, after you have spoken to them for a few minutes, you instinctively know fit the job title 'Fighter Pilot.' You also sense that he belongs in a position of command. You can tell by the way he talks about his experiences and how he relates them to the overall American war effort in Southeast Asia. Gene Tucker did not look upon the Vietnam War as a ticket that had to be punched on the way up the promotional ladder. He saw it as vital to American national interests and he gave it everything he had while on the line. He also kept a diary, which he filled in while waiting in the cockpit of his Phantom during the long 'Alert Five' watches.

The 'Alert Five' watch consisted of fighters which were primed for launch within five minutes of the order being received. The aircraft were armed, positioned on the catapults, with the crews strapped in and starters plugged into the aircraft. As soon as the carrier could be turned into the wind, they could be quickly launched. The purpose of the 'Alert Five' was to intercept any inbound attackers. Because there were never any instances of enemy air attacks against carriers in Vietnam, the 'Alert Five' was usually pretty boring (with one notable exception, which will be related later) and the crews had time to read or write on their watch.

Tucker had two MiG engagements in two combat tours, during which he flew 300 combat missions. He retired as one of the most experienced Navy F-4 pilots, having accumulated over 3,500 hours and over 1,000 'traps' (carrier arrested landings). Upon graduation from the Naval Academy he joined the 'Tincan Navy', even though he fully intended to become a Naval Aviator. This was typical of Gene Tucker's career thinking, even when a young man. He considered an operational knowledge of the 'Blackshoe Navy' essential to his career goals and the best way to gain that knowledge was with actual experience. He finally did get into flight training, just under the age limit. When he got his wings, he attacked the job with equal enthusiasm. His first squadron was VF-33, a newly constituted F-4 squadron, deployed aboard the newest carrier in the Navy at that time, the USS AMERICA (CVA-66). This tour gave him the chance to fly a lot and he finished the tour with over 1,500 hours and 574 'traps.'

His next tour of duty was at the Naval Air Test Center, Patuxent River, Maryland. After graduating from Test Pilot School, he reported to the Carrier Suitability Branch of the Flight Test Division, where he did takeoff, approach, and landing tests. He was heavily involved in the Automatic Carrier Landing System project and in the Navy's first testing of the Grumman F-14A Tomcat.

From Pax River he reported to VF-103 as Operations Officer, making a Med cruise aboard USS SARATOGA (CVA-60). Upon return, he was assigned as Officer in Charge (OIC) of the VF-101 Air Combat Maneuvering (ACM) Detachment at Naval Air Station (NAS) Key West. After a year of ACM at Key West, he reported to VF-74 for his XO/CO tour. That tour was good for two Med cruises, one on USS NIMITZ (CVN-68) and one on USS FORRESTAL (CVA-59). He was then assigned as Commander Air Group (CAG) on FORRESTAL, flying most of his missions with VF-11 and VF-74. A tour as Commander of Fighter Wing One at NAS Oceana followed, and it was during this tour that one of his squadrons bagged two Libyan Sukhoi Su 17 Fitter fighters (VF-41 F-14 Tomcats over the Gulf of Sidra during 1981). He commanded two ships, including a supply ship and then a carrier, the USS CORAL SEA (CVA-43) before retiring and...as he euphemistically puts it; "going to work for a living." Like so many professional military aviators, he did not want to give up flying. Right up to the last couple of assignments in the Navy, he had been able to have his regular 'flying fix.' When he retired he wanted to fly for an airline, but he didn't want to just fly aircraft. His last 13 years in the Navy had been spent in positions of command and he wanted to have some say in the day-to-day operations of whatever outfit he went with.

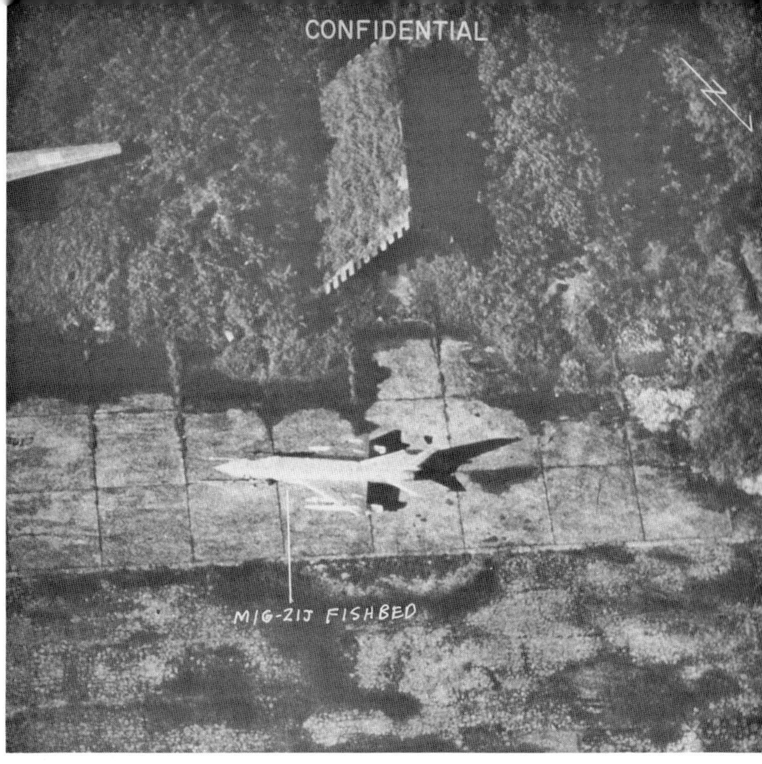

North Vietnamese opposition to the Phantom was the MiG-17, MiG-19 and MiG-21. This Fishbed J, parked in a revetment at Hanoi Gia Lam airfield on 3 September 1972, is armed with Atoll AAMs on the inboard wing pylons and has external fuel tanks on the outboard pylons. (U.S. Air Force)

Gene Tucker joined Presidential Airways during 1985 and quickly checked out in the Boeing 737. He had chosen Presidential, a new airline operating from Dulles International, near Washington, D.C., because he would have the opportunity to work in management while flying. He ran their charter operations, then moved to systems operations where he currently holds the title of Vice President. His operational diary, while flying combat cruises with VF-33 and VF-103, provided the background information for his accounts of operations on the line and the details of his two MiG engagements. They are reprinted here with his permission.

One of the southernmost MiG airfields in North Vietnam was Vinh, although MiGs were rarely stationed there for any length of time. This mosaic, prepared by shipboard photographic interpreters, shows the damage to Vinh airfield after it was attacked and cratered during the Linebacker campaign of 1972. (Tucker)

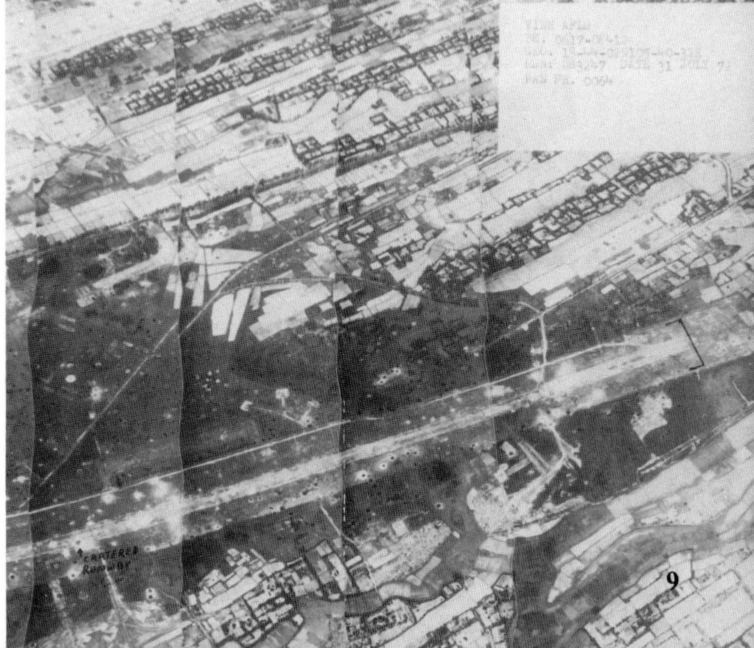

CARRIER OPERATIONS DURING THE VIETNAM WAR

CAPT R.E. TUCKER, Jr., USN (Ret)

The catapult crew aboard USS MIDWAY check the catapult tow bridle attached to this F-4B of VF-151 on the port bow catapult. USS MIDWAY (CVA-41) was operating in the South China Sea on Yankee Station during August of 1964. (U.S. Navy)

The attack carriers of the US Navy were the mainstay of the air war against North Vietnam throughout the Vietnam war. There were generally three to five carriers in theater at any one time; with five being the usual during the 71-72 time frame. Typically there would be one carrier on Dixie Station and two to three on Yankee Station. Dixie Station was about 70 nautical miles due east of Cam Ranh Bay, South Vietnam. Yankee Station was about 70-100 nautical miles east of Vinh, North Vietnam, with both stations being within the Gulf of Tonkin. Carriers frequently tracked north of Vinh up to a position east of Thanh Hoa and occasionally as far north as just east of Haiphong, but always at least 70 nautical miles at sea to reduce the threat of attack from North Vietnamese MiGs. I heard that on one occasion, during a period of major strikes against Hanoi and Haiphong, one carrier came to within 30-50 nautical miles of Haiphong.

There was also one carrier in transit to or from ports such as Subic Bay, The Philippines (the norm), Yokosuka, Japan (once a cruise), and Hong Kong (once a cruise). Enroute to WESTPAC (Western Pacific), West Coast based carriers would stop in Hawaii and East Coast based carriers might stop in Rio de Janeiro, Brazil. On the way back to CONUS a lucky carrier might get a port call in Australia or New Zealand. For several years (66-68 and 71-72) after the last line period, 60 to 70 percent of the air wing aircrews would get to fly home early, on a 'Magic Carpet' flight out of Cubi Point, The Philippines. This was due to the the length of the cruises (typically nine to ten months) and the short turn-around cycle. Six months was normally spent in CONUS, but frequently as much as three months of this 'at home' time was spent away from home on shore-based training detachments, or at sea during REFTRA (Refresher Training) or TYT/ORE (Type Training/Operational Readiness Evaluations) for the next cruise.

A pair of Phantoms of VF-142 and VF-143 dump fuel prior to landing aboard USS CONSTELLATION on 3 September 1964. The dumping of fuel was necessary to lower the aircraft's weight to within safe limits before landing. (U.S. Navy)

There were several classes of aircraft carriers involved in the Vietnam War. The oldest and by far the smallest, were what we called '27 Charlie class' carriers, converted from straight deck carriers of Second World War vintage. These included USS INTREPID (CV-11), USS HANCOCK (CV-19), USS BON HOMME RICHARD (CVA-31), and USS ORISKANY (CV-34). Most of these carriers were phased out by 1970. The air wing on a 27 Charlie included two fighter squadrons of F-8 Crusaders, two or three light attack A-4 Skyhawk squadrons, one attack squadron of A-1 Skyraiders, an airborne early warning squadron of E-1B Tracers, and plane guard helicopter detachments. Some carriers also carried a detachment of photo F-8s for reconnaissance missions. Although small in size, the 27 Charlie carriers and their air wings bore the brunt of the early air war in Vietnam and their F-8 fighters scored most of the Navy's MiG kills prior to 1970.

The more modern MIDWAY class carriers, designed after the Second World War, were built with an angled deck and were larger in size than the 27 Charlies. MIDWAY class carriers could handle the F-4 Phantom which were too heavy for operations from the 27 Charlies. The class consisted of USS MIDWAY (CVA-41), USS FRANKLIN D ROOSEVELT (CVA-42), and USS CORAL SEA (CVA-43). The basic air wing composition was much like that of the smaller CVs, but included two squadrons of F-4B Phantoms, which replaced the F-8s as they were phased out. Additionally, Grumman E-2B Hawkeyes replaced the E-1B Tracers in the Early Warning business and Grumman A-6 Intruders took over the medium attack mission from the A-1 Skyraiders.

The supercarriers were the largest class of carriers and were a quantum leap in size and capability over the MIDWAY class ships. Although all carriers from USS FORRESTAL (CVA-59) on were considered supercarriers, there were actually several classes within that grouping. USS FORRESTAL (CVA-59), USS SARATOGA (CVA-60), USS RANGER (CVA-61), and USS INDEPENDENCE (CVA-62) were the same (i.e. FORRESTAL) class. USS KITTY HAWK (CVA-63) and USS CONSTELLATION (CVA-64) were the same (i.e. KITTY HAWK) class. USS ENTERPRISE (CVAN-65) was the only nuclear-powered carrier used in the war and USS AMERICA (CVA-66) was the newest carrier to see action in Vietnam, making deployments in 1968, 1970, and 1972. All subsequent supercarriers were constructed too late to see action in Vietnam.

The supercarriers had a more versatile air wing composition, consisting of two fighter squadrons of twelve F-4 Phantoms each, two light attack squadrons of twelve Vought A-7 Corsair IIs each, one medium attack squadron of ten A-6 Intruder all-weather bombers and four or five KA-6D tankers, one early warning squadron of four E-2B Hawkeyes, one reconnaissance squadron of six Rockwell RA-5C Vigilantes, and one helo squadron of eight SH-3 Sea Kings. Frequently supercarriers would also carry a two or three aircraft detachment of Douglas KA-3 Skywarrior tankers or EKA-3 electronic jammer/tankers and a two to four aircraft detachment of the HH-3 or HH-53 'Big Mother' Search and Rescue (SAR) helos.

During the first year or two of the war, Navy aircraft had no radar warning or Electronic Counter Measures (ECM) devices. In about 1966/67 a unit called 'Big Ear' was used for a short time. This was a small, plug-in unit that was held to the inside of the canopy by a suction cup and gave an aural warning that you were being illuminated by radar, but did not include type of radar or bearing. By 1968 we had much better systems which gave threat type and bearing. We also had some jamming capability and the ability to drop Chaff to assist in protection against radar tracking. Flares were also used to help evade infrared homing missiles.

The staff of Commander, Carrier Task Force 77 (CTF 77) rode one of the carriers on Yankee Station and ran the Naval Air War. Their mission was to coordinate the schedules and efforts of all the carriers. Each carrier conducted flight operations for twelve hours and had the next twelve hours to conduct maintenance (called Cyclic Operations). During the twelve hours of air operations, the normal routine was to launch a group of aircraft every hour and a half, or on some carriers, every hour and forty-five minutes. The cycles were numbered consecutively, starting with the first launch so that on the noon to midnight schedule, the first cycle launched at noon, the second at 1330 (The first cycle aircraft recovering immediately after the second cycle launched.) Each squadron was assigned an event number on each cycle. One fighter squadron would always be designated by A, so that its events would be identified 1A, 2A, 3A, etc. The other fighter squadron's events would be 1B, 2B, 3B, etc; the first A-7 squadron would be 1C, 2C, 3C and so on through all the squadrons of the air wing.

An average daytime launch would consist of six fighters, six-eight light attack aircraft, two-four medium attack, two-three tankers, an E-2B, one RA-5C, and one EKA-3. A plane guard helicopter was always airborne during launches and recoveries. Yankee Station carrier flight operations were scheduled to keep continuous pressure on the North Vietnamese. Typically one carrier would fly from noon to midnight and another would take over and fly from midnight to noon. If there were a third carrier on Yankee Station, its flight hours would generally overlap, possibly from 0600-1800 (typically the smaller carrier flew more daylight hours, especially as more and more big-deck carriers arrived on the scene).

Instead of cyclic ops, the third carrier might be assigned to conduct 'Alpha Strikes' against selected targets in North Vietnam. On this schedule a Carrier Air Wing would generally launch three Alpha Strikes a day; one early morning, one around noon, and one mid to late afternoon. An 'Alpha Strike' would typically consist of forty to forty-five aircraft; eight to ten fighters as Combat Air Patrol (CAP) or strike/escort, twelve to fourteen light attack, four to six medium attack, two E-2Bs to assist in vectors to the coast-in points and to keep count of those coasting-in and those safely 'feet wet', three-five tankers for the fighters (besides the KA-6D, we also used the A-7 with a D-704 Buddy store to augment the tanker assets), one to two RA-5C Vigilantes for Bomb Damage Assessment (BDA), each with a fighter escort, and two to six A-7 and A-6 Anti-Radiation (ARM) missile configured aircraft capable of launching Shrike or Standard ARM missiles against Surface to Air Missile (SAM) or Anti-Aircraft Artillery (AAA) sites. Occasionally, especially in 1972, all three carriers would be on a three Alpha Strike schedule for several days in a row. The targets and the time on target would be coordinated so that, although each carrier had separate targets, the support forces such as MIGCAP or photo birds could cover two carriers strikes because the targets would be geographically close together (twenty miles or less) and time on target was within five-ten minutes of one another. We carefully chose routes that avoided having one strike group enroute to the target and another strike group coming off the target (heading for the Gulf) from meeting each other head-on. We also avoided having a strike group fly through another carrier's target area enroute to its own target.

Hanoi SAM site (target number VN159) was typical of SA-2 Guideline sites spread throughout North Vietnam. The SA-2 was one of the most feared anti-aircraft weapons in Vietnam, although in terms of actual hits, it was the least effective. It was 34 feet 9 inches long, weighed two and a half tons, with a maximum speed of Mach 3.5, and a range of 25 miles. American pilots learned to defeat the SA-2... if they saw it launch and were able to determine if it was locked on. The technique required waiting until the SAM was close, than break hard into it. If you broke too soon, the SAM stayed locked on; too late — it exploded close enough to be lethal. (U.S. Navy)

The catapult officer aboard USS CORAL SEA (CVA-43) signals the pilot of this F-4B of VF-51 to go to full power during air operations on 4 October 1965. When the Phantom reaches full power the catapult officer will signal for the catapult to fire, launching the Phantom from the deck. (U.S. Navy)

Deployments to Vietnam were normally nine-ten months long. Occasionally one would be eight months or eleven months, but that was unusual. Each deployment was divided into five-six line periods, normally thirty-five to forty-five days long, but occasionally they lasted sixty or even ninety to one hundred days if things got too hot, or a relieving carrier had problems. After a line period, a carrier would get ten to fourteen days off the line, part of it spent proceeding to or from port and actually spending five to ten days in port for maintenance and R&R (rest and recreation). While 'on the line' a carrier would 'stand down' for one day every six to twelve days. Normally after the stand down would come a shift of the cyclic schedule — if the carrier had been on the midnight to noon, they would take over the noon to midnight schedule after the 'stand down'.

Dixie Station aircraft worked in support of operations south of the DMZ. A carrier would normally spend the first line period, or at least the first two weeks of the first line period, on Dixie Station. Here the Air Group would work in a lower threat environment while indoctrinating new pilots and smoothing the bugs out of Air Wing procedures and tactics. The A-4 Skyhawks (replaced during the 1968-71 time frame by the A-7 Corsair II), the A-6 Intruders, and the F-4 Phantom all carried MK-80 series bombs (usually MK-82 500 pounders) and rockets (2.75 inch FFAR and 5 inch Zunis) in support of ground operations on close air support missions. We normally worked under the control of a Forward Air Controller (FAC) or Fast FAC on a specific target. The FAC normally marked the target with smoke rockets fired from his aircraft. Occasionally we would join on a LORAN or Radar Beacon equipped USAF F-4 and fly his wing for a multi-aircraft bomb release. This was normally done in overcast weather when visual target acquisition was not possible.

The major portion of the Naval Air War in Vietnam was fought from the decks of the carriers on Yankee Station against targets north of the DMZ. North Vietnam was subdivided into various geographic sections, called 'Route Packages.' The Navy had primary responsibility for targets in Route Packages II (an area from the Gulf to the Laotion border centered roughly around Vinh), IV (around Thanh Hoa) and VI-A (Haiphong to Hanoi). The Air Force had primary responsibility for Route Packages I, III, V, and VI-B. In fact, although we rarely worked in each others Route Packages, we both worked a great deal around the Hanoi target area. Some of the primary missions which Navy F-4 aircraft flew included strike missions, Target Combat Air Patrol (TARCAP), Barrier Combat Air Patrol (BARCAP), MiG Combat Air Patrol (MIGCAP), and photo escort.

Armed with bombs on the outboard wing plyons, an F-4B of VF-41 Black Aces is launched from USS INDEPENDENCE (CVA-62) for an air strike against targets in North Vietnam on 26 July 1965. (U.S. Navy)

The Navy flew a lot of strike missions (air-to-ground ordnance delivery) of various types and the F-4 certainly flew its share with varying weapons loads. Commander Task Force 77 would receive a daily frag message from 7th Air Force HQ in Saigon and the targets would then be assigned to the various carriers by the CTF-77 staff. Small targets such as a group of WBLCs (Water-borne Logistics Craft) or a truck park would be assigned to an individual squadron for a given event. These missions were generally flown in a two aircraft section, although occasionally a division of four F-4s would work a target together. Sometimes a section of F-4s would go to a target with a section or division of A-7s. Even if not working the same target, several sections (whose targets were in close proximity) might go in together for mutual navigation benefits (Navy F-4Bs and F-4Js did not have Inertial Nav Systems), to provide some fighter cover for the light attack birds, or just to avoid meeting each other head-on enroute to or from the target area.

F-4 weapons loads on strike missions varied considerably depending on the target composition and specific ordnance availability. Cluster Bomb Units (CBUs) — good against trucks, armored vehicles, and for flak suppression were frequently in low supply. F-4s always carried a bag of missiles, usually two AIM-7E Sparrows mounted on the aft fuselage stations, and two-four AIM-9 Sidewinders on wing stations two and/or eight. Navy F-4s had no internal gun and almost never carried the 20MM MK-4 gunpod because it was extremely unreliable and could only be carried on the centerline (station five), where we liked to carry our external fuel tank; as opposed to USAF F-4s which normally carried two wing fuel tanks. We would carry TERs (triple ejector racks) on stations one and nine (outboard wing stations) or two and eight (inboard wing stations) as standard, although when carrying a mixed ordnance load such as bombs and rockets, or bombs and flares we would carry a TER on each of the four stations. Our most common bomb load was six MK-82 LDGP bombs. When working south of the DMZ we carried napalm, more so in the early years of the war. When carrying the

An F-4B of VF-114 Aardvarks is positioned in its parking spot aboard USS KITTY HAWK (CVA-63) after returning from strikes against North Vietnam during February of 1966. VF-114 was the first operational West Coast Phantom squadron, receiving its aircraft in July of 1961. (U.S. Navy)

MK-80 series bombs we frequently had both nose and tail fuzing to provide airborne flexibility. A mechanical fuze preset with the arming delay and detonation delay which was best for the intended target would be in the nose. The tail fuze was electrical and the detonation delay could be selected in flight by the pilot. This enabled the pilot to select, in flight, a shorter time delay or instantaneous detonation for a soft target if the mechanical fuze had been preset for a long delay against a hard target and your mission was changed or you had to go to an alternate target due to weather.

When a target was assigned, the flight leader would assemble the flight to plan the mission. Each carrier had a CVIC (Carrier Intelligence Center) with as many as eight-ten Intelligence Officers as well as enlisted specialists in Data Processing (DPs), Photography (PHs), Data Systems Technicians (DSs), and Photographic Intelligencemen (PTs). The CVIC was equipped with computers to maintain current enemy anti-aircraft and MiG Order of Battle information. This information was briefed to the aircrews as well as being displayed on large charts along with target data and photographs required to plan the mission. Ingress and egress routes and ordnance delivery parameters would be decided upon, photos of the target obtained (if available), and each crewmember would mark the intended routes on his personal chart.

The typical strike mission flown by Navy F-4s was characterized by a half hour to forty-five minutes of very busy activity followed by forty-five minutes of boring 'Max Conserve' holding while awaiting recovery aboard the carrier. Immediately after launch, the F-4s would join with a tanker, usually overhead the carrier, but frequently enroute to the coast-in point. Each Phantom would take on 2,000 pounds of fuel. The flight would then proceed to the target to drop their ordnance early in the cycle because of the high fuel consumption of the F-4 while carrying bombs or rocket pods. For the same reason we normally had a specific target assigned, although occasionally we would be assigned to recce a segment of road looking for targets of opportunity.

We virtually always flew in a combat spread formation — wingman within 10 degrees of abeam, at a mile to a mile and a half and stepped up 1,500 to 2,500 feet. We would fly to the coast at medium altitude (15,000 feet) and 300 knots, accelerating to 400 knots or more as we coasted-in. Altitudes varied between air wings, target location, and period of the war. Generally the altitude varied between 10,000 to 18,000 feet. Typically we would descend from 15,000 to 12,000 feet and accelerate when about 5-10 miles from the coast. At the target we generally used a high angle dive delivery for better accuracy, more speed, and less vulnerability to AAA. The parameters for the F-4 were a 40-45 degree dive angle, rolling in from about 11,000 feet, with weapons release at 5,000 to 6,000 feet at 500 knots. Most pilots dropped the six bombs in the ripple mode, but I preferred three quick pickles in 'bombs pairs'. When flying in a section, only one aircraft would make his bomb run at a time so that someone else would be watching for flak, keeping the 'big picture', and at least would be able to say what happened if you took a hit during your run. Usually the leader, who navigated to the target, rolled in first, with the wingman rolling in as lead pulled off the target. This would change the wingman's roll-in heading anywhere from 45 to 180 degrees from that of the leader. The section would then head for the Gulf, slowly climbing, mildly jinking, and keeping 400 knots or better airspeed. We advertised 3,500 feet as the minimum altitude over the beach in order to stay out of small arms range. (I personally feel that 70% or more of the Naval Aviators who got bagged by AAA were violating one or more of the known precepts of combat in Vietnam.) The basic rules were simple: (1) Don't get low or slow. (2) Stay above 3,500 feet. (3) No more than one run on the target. (4) Subsequent aircraft should not fly down the leader's flight path to the target. (5) Jink.

After 'coast-out', the section would slow to about 250 knots, join up in cruise formation, looking each other over for any combat damage, climb to 18-20,000 feet, and hold near the carrier at maximum endurance airspeed (about 100 pounds of fuel per minute) until the recovery (scheduled landing) time. We would have liked to climb to 25-30,000 feet for fuel conservation, but the Air Force owned the airspace above 20,000 feet, even over the Gulf, and we rarely flew above 20,000 feet.

On Alpha Strikes, the F-4s could be assigned as strike aircraft, TARCAP (Target CAP), or MIGCAP. The only difference between strike F-4s and TARCAP F-4s was that after bomb release the TARCAP would remain in the target vicinity until the last aircraft released ordnance, then would follow the strike group out. The weapons load was the same. Frequently strike F-4s would be used as flak suppressors, proceeding to the target with the strike group, but accelerating ahead when one-two minutes from the target to drop flak suppression ordnance, such as CBUs, Rockeye, or VT fuzed MK-83 bombs on active or known AAA sites before the strike aircraft rolled in.

Two other strike missions, which F-4s flew, were Laser Guided Bomb (LGB) flights and mining operations. We did both missions during 1972. The F-4, because of the two seat tandem cockpit arrangement, was best suited to the LGB designator mission. We were using a hand-held LGB designator which looked somewhat like a Brownie camera. The designator aircraft would proceed to the target with the strike aircraft (normally a section of A-7s, although occasionally an F-4 would carry LGBs - a normal MK-82, 83, or 84 fitted with a Laser-Seeker head and guidance fins.) The strike aircraft would put their ordnance in the air while the designator aircraft flew a steady semi-circle around the target, with the RIO illuminating the target with his hand-held designator. Hits were good, but this system was not healthy in a high threat environment, such as Hanoi, because the designator aircraft flew a predictable flight path and both the pilot and the RIO were padlocked (paying 100% visual

Armed with a napalm tank on the outboard wing pylon, this F-4B Phantom of VF-213 Black Lions is enroute to targets in South Vietnam during February of 1966. VF-213 was sister squadron to VF-114 and part of Air Wing Eleven (CVW-11) aboard USS KITTY HAWK. (U.S. Navy)

attention) to the target.

When the Navy was dropping mines, the F-4s were right in there. We carried six MK-82 bombs with snakeye fins, configured as mines with influence fuzes. Since the Navy F-4 did not have an inertial navigation system (INS), it could not navigate with the precision required for laying an accurate minefield and we always flew on the wing of an A-6 during mining operations. On these missions, we flew at low altitudes both while approaching the target and during delivery, since the entire flight was over water. The formation would be at 200 to 400 feet to ensure release accuracy and reduce exposure to SAMs and AAA.

Most carriers had their own reconnaissance aircraft, either photo F-8s or RA-5C Vigilantes. There would be a photo bird airborne on each cycle, getting updated target photos, doing reconnaissance of road segments, or getting Bomb Damage Assessments (BDA) photos. During major strike evolutions two Vigilantes would be assigned to get BDA. Each photo bird would have a photo escort, because the Vigilante was unarmed and highly vulnerable to enemy defenses while on a photo run. Photo escort missions were extremely interesting. The F-4 escort would get a big shot of fuel after launch (around 5,000 pounds) and would sometimes require an additional 2,000 pounds after coasting out, depending on the length of the photo run. The RA-5C flight profile varied, but typically the mission was flown around 3,500 to 5,000 feet and at low supersonic speeds (Mach 1-1.2). These speeds were in the 'high drag rise' regime of flight for the F-4, so we used a lot of fuel. The photo escort had to work to keep up with the sleek Vigilante, which had no trouble accelerating to, or holding 1.2 Mach. Additionally, the Vigilante usually flew 'clean', while the Phantom escort carried drag producing pylons, missiles, and external fuel tanks. The photo escort generally positioned themselves one mile abeam of the photo bird, stepped up, and looking towards the most significant threat area. While navigating and taking pictures, the Vigilante crew (pilot and NFO) devoted much of their attention inside the cockpit. Even when looking outside, their field of view was limited by the design of the Vigilante. Escorts reported flak or SAMs which were threatening because the Vigilante crew didn't (couldn't) see the threat.

The hands-down favorite F-4 mission for all fighter jocks was MIGCAP. During the early years of the war (pre-1969), a carrier would occasionally position a MIGCAP section of F-4s feet wet just off the coast, or have them transit North Vietnam somewhere between 18 and 19 degrees north latitude to take up station inside Laos, where they could react quickly to any MiGs which came up to challenge cyclic ops. Later, especially in 1972, MIGCAPs were used only in connection with major Navy strikes (Alpha Strikes) or joint evolutions such as B-52 bombing raids. At least two, and sometimes as many as four, sections of MIGCAP were assigned to cover Alpha Strikes. Each MIGCAP section would be assigned a geographic section of North Vietnam, normally somewhere between the target and the closest known MiG base.

MIGCAP aircraft would launch early in the Alpha Strike cycle. Each section usually had its own KA-6D tanker assigned and would rendezvous with the tanker before proceeding towards the coast-in point. The flight leader would have computed the exact time he would have to coast-in in order to be into position to provide protection as the strike group proceeded to the target and to be on the assigned MIGCAP station a few minutes prior to the time the strike arrived on target. Keeping this in mind, he would have to decide when to commence refueling the fighters so they could get as much of their assigned fuel as possible (usually 5,000-6,000 pounds for each F-4) and be finished tanking at least 10 miles off the coast (there was no sense in taking the tankers any closer to the threat than necessary). He had to allow enough time for tanking while still make his computed coast-in time.

The fighter section would coast-in at a good speed - 400 knots or better, usually at a medium altitude — 10,000 to 15,000 feet, and proceed to station. The section's mission was not to jump any MiGs they could get their hands on, but to intercept any MiGs that posed a threat to the strike group. Sometimes that was hard to remember because fighter jocks naturally like to go for the first MiG they see or hear about. This tendency could, however, get you suckered into chasing MiGs 50 miles from the strike group, which would render the strike aircraft vulnerable to other MiGs. The flight leader had to evaluate each situation and make his decisions on the information available, which was not always plentiful.

One of the consistent problems facing MIGCAP (other than the fact that the stations were usually in high threat areas, with lots of AAA, SAMs and MiGs) was that their CAP control frequency was always different from the frequency assigned to the strike group. Since Navy F-4s only had one radio, the CAP had to depend on the controller to pass on info regarding the progress of the strike group. It was not unusual to have the MIGCAP air controller so engrossed in his hunt for MiGs and control of the CAP that he would forget that the MIGCAP were only required to cover the strike group. I remember several times when I felt like we had been on station an unusually long time, dodging SAMs and AAA. I would ask the controller how much longer until the strike group got to the target only to be told; "Oh, they hit the target five minutes ago." That usually meant there was no one around to protect anymore and since I didn't see much sense in getting any more practice at dodging SAMs than was absolutely necessary, we would head 'feet wet'!

During 1972, when Navy A-6s were making a number of single aircraft low-level night strikes all over the area between Haiphong and Hanoi, MiGs were known to launch, making the A-6 drivers nervous (although I personally felt that the MiGs had no night/IFR capability against an A-6 at 300 feet). As a result, we started position-

An F-4B of VF-142 Ghostriders dumps fuel as it enters the downwind leg for approach and landing aboard USS CONSTELLATION after returning from a 15 July 1967 mission over North Vietnam. (U.S. Navy)

ing a single F-4 on MIGCAP along the coastline at night. We figured a single F-4 didn't have to worry about a mid-air with his wingman and had plenty of potential at night against a single MiG. If a MiG launched and headed towards an A-6, the F-4 would vector for the MiG. Invariably MiGs would run for home when the F-4 got to within 25-30 miles of them. Some fighter pilots weren't too overjoyed about the night MIGCAP missions, but I personally felt it was a golden opportunity and my MiG kill proved it. I figured that the MiG had a negligible opportunity to do anyone bodily harm at night with his limited weapons system and Atoll/guns load, whereas the F-4 had a good solid head-on or tail shot against any MiG he could find and get close enough to shoot at. I also liked the fact that the dark eliminated visually guided AAA or SAMs, so if your ECM equipment was working, you at least knew someone was shooting at you, and you could see flak and tracers much better at night. I admit it wasn't any fun at all dodging SAMs at night, especially with the reduction in depth perception in the dark. I've expended a lot of energy dodging SAMs that I later realized were probably fired at someone 5 or 10 miles away from me! We also flew the single F-4 night MIGCAP in support of the USAF night B-52 raids over North Vietnam during 1972. I've always had the greatest respect for those B-52 crews because I spent many a night on MIGCAP station watching as those lumbering giants unleashed their fury on the North Vietnamese, only to be targeted by hundreds of SAMs. It is not a pretty sight to watch one of those B-52s fall from the sky in flames.

While MIGCAP missions were the most exciting and sought after, BARCAP was the most boring. The Barrier CAP (BARCAP) station was manned continuously by a section of fighters throughout the war. The station was about a 20 mile long racetrack oriented parallel to the coast and about 20 miles feet wet southeast of Haiphong. The purpose of the BARCAP was to defend against any surprise MiG attack against any US ships (Red Crown or the north SAR) or against any of the 'spook' (USAF recce) aircraft which ran along a north/south track well off the coast of northern North Vietnam (such as the 'Big Look' EC-121).

The BARCAP normally launched fifteen minutes prior to the scheduled launch, since the station was some 125 miles from the carrier. The F-4 section would launch, take on 2,000 pounds of fuel each from the tanker, then head north to station. Relief on station was required. The section would hold at 270 - 300 knots, flying a combat spread or (at night or IFR) a two mile radar trail formation at 15,000 to 18,000 feet. 99 percent of the time there was nothing going on, but once in a blue moon an unidentified radar contact would pop up and cause some concern on the north SAR ship or Red Crown and the BARCAP would be vectored to investigate. Most of the time it would prove to be weather, however, several missiles were fired by the BARCAP during the war at night at what was thought to be high speed surface contacts (possibly Komar missile boats), helos, An 2 Colt biplanes, and even a MiG or two. I believe a confirmed Colt, a possible Colt, and a possible MiG were credited to BARCAP fighters during the course of the war. Not much excitement for eight years of patrolling! About forty-five minutes to an hour after arriving on station, the BARCAP tanker would show up and give each F-4 another 3,000 - 5,000 pounds of fuel. This kept them loaded with a decent 2,000 pound combat package of fuel throughout the cycle. When the relief BARCAP section showed up and you were released, you would stroke it for the carrier, using your 'combat package' fuel for a quick One V One training engagement, and then to hustle back to the carrier at 500 knots or more (frequently supersonic). The BARCAP were always the last aircraft in the cycle to recover because of the distance they had to travel. The carrier had to steam into the wind, normally at 20 knots or more (there wasn't a lot of natural wind in the Gulf) until all aircraft were recovered. More than one BARCAP flight leader had to personally debrief the Captain or Admiral on the reason why 5,000 people had to steam into the wind while the BARCAP section was doing a tailchase or hassle on the way back to the carrier!

No matter how boring or exciting your mission was, or what condition you or the aircraft was in when you returned, at the end of each flight you knew you had to get it back on deck...day or night, good weather or bad. The nearest divert field was Danang, some 200 nautical miles from Yankee Station, which was too great a distance for an F-4 which had burned his fuel down to maximum gross landing weight. Each aircraft type has a maximum gross landing weight at which it can safely 'trap' aboard the carrier. That weight is made up of the aircraft's basic weight plus the weight of the stores carried and the fuel on board. In the period before 1970, the F-4 with a normal missile and bomb rack (TER) load, frequently had to have less than 3,500 pounds of fuel to land and sometimes as little as 2,200 pounds. A typical night landing pattern took 800 pounds, so there wasn't much gravy. In the 1970's, the max trap fuel weight was raised to 5,800 pounds, although you rarely had that much after a mission.

Once your mission was over, typically within forty-five minutes of launch (for the F-4s), you had forty-five to sixty minutes to max conserve and think about the carrier landing ahead. A carrier landing has to be seen to appreciate what it's like to hurl your 40,000 pound F-4 at the back end of a carrier at 145 knots, especially at night or in bad weather. It is a tribute to the pilots and the Landing Signal Officers (LSOs) that we are highly successful in that regard, and have had relatively few landing accidents. In a controlled study done during the war, a number of Naval Aviators were wired to record pulse and respiration rates during typical combat missions. These rates were found to be consistently higher during operations around the boat than they were in combat, proving that, to a Naval Aviator, the routine job is the most exciting part of any mission.

F-4B of VF-21 Freelancers releases its bombs in the ripple mode during a 3 November 1965 air strike over North Vietnam. VF-21 was operating from USS MIDWAY (CVA-41) on Yankee Station. (U.S. Navy)

OBSERVATIONS ON THE WAR

"Throughout the war, Naval Aviators were extremely upset about the political limitations imposed upon them. At various times entire geographical areas were off limits and there was always a list of specific target restrictions. Everyone could agree with limitations obviously designed to protect from the massive and indiscriminate killing of civilians, however, at varying times virtually every type of war fighting machinery, military facility, or industrial capacity was placed 'off limits'. I failed to see the logic behind fighting a war without permission to bomb MiG airfields, army barracks, and most amazing to me...SAM sites!

I was aboard SARATOGA during her last combat cruise from May of 1972 to January of 1973. I was Fighter Squadron 103 (VF-103) Operations Officer throughout the cruise and simultaneously held the Air Wing Operations Officer job from September of 1972 on because the incumbent was shot down. Things got hot and heavy towards the end and we loved the pressure of the B-52 strikes and the many '3 Alpha' (three Alpha Strikes per day) days by the carriers on Yankee Station. We felt we were working them over good, but the price was high. We were losing quite a number of aircraft, particularly A-6s. Our A-6 squadron, VA-75, lost two commanding officers during the cruise and so many aircrews that towards the end of the deployment they had four crews who were instructors in the East Coast Replacement Air Group (RAG - VA-42) assigned on TAD (TDY). Several of these TAD crews were also bagged.

It was terribly aggravating to be ordered to back off whenever the North Vietnamese hinted at peace talks. It was more upsetting to give them a two to four week breather in the Hanoi/Haiphong area to rebuild defenses and resupply SAMs and AAA ammo and then have to go back hard at it, right to Hanoi, overnight. I always thought it would have saved a lot of our people and hurt them a lot more in the end, to go back into a full-swing air war in a more logical manner. I would have liked to see us start right at the coast and take on every active SAM site and airfield, successively eliminating them as a threat. Then work our way inland, laying waste to their war-making capacity along the way. Instead we seemed to go at it in a haphazard way, alternately applying heavy pressure then backing off, generally at the mercy of political desires in targeting instead of military reality.

I personally felt a lot of pride in the accomplishments of SARATOGA and Carrier Air Wing Three and I felt good about the contributions of the Navy and the Air Force within the many continuous political constraints imposed. I could see what was coming, however, at the time of the cease-fire. We had not beaten the North Vietnamese to their knees, militarily or psychologically. We could have and should have, once we chose to get involved in the first place. The only good thing about the cease-fire was that we got the POWs out. They had been miserably treated.

I am not ashamed to say that, as I later sat at home and watched newscasts of the evacuation of Saigon as it was being overrun by the communists from the north, I cried. What a terrible waste of the years of effort and the countless American lives. What a loss of face to our allies and boost to our enemies. The politicians could justify it or wordsmith their way around it anyway they wanted, but there was no doubt in my mind that the United States of America had just lost its first war."

Phantoms of VF-14 Tophatters launch from USS FRANKLIN D. ROOSEVELT (CVA-42) for a strike against North Vietnam on 14 November 1966. The Vietnamese fishing vessel off the port bow sailed across the FDR's bow during the launch in an attempt to disrupt flight operations. (U.S. Navy)

An F-4 of VF-143 Puking Dogs in the three fuel tank configuration used for long over land missions into Laos and Cambodia. The fin tip and fuel tank tips are in Red. (Jim Hurley)

Guy Freeborn

...had plenty of experience in fighters before making his first combat cruise. He had previously flown two cruises in the F3H Demon, the McDonnell fighter that preceded the Phantom II, and had spent three years as an instructor in VF-121, the West Coast Phantom Replacement Air Group (RAG). This was before 'Top Gun', however, ACM was coming back into vogue and Freeborn had come to know the Phantom's air combat strengths and weaknesses before he took it into combat.

Freeborn was number two in a flight of VF-142 Phantoms that were led by LCDR Bob Davis, with LCDR Gayle 'Swede' Elie as his back seater. Freeborn's RIO was LTJG Bob Elliot. The flight launched from USS CONSTELLATION (CVA-64) at 1145 on 10 August 1967. They were assigned TARCAP for a series of multiple strikes against the Phu Ly Transshipment Point. The strike aircraft were to launch from two carriers, the CONSTELLATION and USS INTREPID (CVA-11).

The Phantoms hit their tanker prior to coasting in, refueled, and headed north with a full bag of fuel. Each F-4 was armed with a pair of AIM-7 Sparrows and four AIM-9 Sidewinders. They reached their assigned CAP station, the foothills west of Nam Dinh and, in loose combat spread formation, began a random left hand orbit at 16,000 feet. There was an overcast at 22,000 feet. Because the GCI-directed MiGs were expected to attack from above, where they would have the advantage of building speed in a dive, the Phantom pilots had opted for the lower altitude. From below they hoped to be able to spot the MiGs as they dropped out of the overcast. The MiGs would be the most visible at that time and also the most vulnerable; since the MiG pilots would be in the disorienting transition from instruments to visual flight.

The CONSTELLATION strike group hit Phu Ly at 1230. From their CAP station, Davis and Freeborn were able to observe some of the activity. As the strike group pulled off the target and headed for the coast, the MiGs appeared. Davis and Freeborn had heard several earlier MiG calls from Red Crown, however, none of them had affected their mission. The CONNIE's bombers were now out of the target area, but there was still no sign of INTREPID's group. Navy Phantoms only had one radio and they had theirs tuned to the CONSTELLATION strike frequency. They quickly switched to INTREPID's frequency, but their repeated calls went unanswered. They finally gave up and switched back to CONSTELLATION's frequency (they would later learn that INTREPID had weather-aborted their mission). After assuring that the CONSTELLATION strike group was safely 'feet wet', they once again tuned to the INTREPID's frequency.

MiG killers LCDR Gayle Elie, LCDR Robert Davis, LT Guy Freeborn, and ENS Robert Elliot of VF-142 aboard USS CONSTELLATION after their twin MiG kill on 8 October 1967. (U.S. Navy)

An F-4B Phantom of VF-14 on a MIGCAP mission over the Gulf of Tonkin on 6 December 1966. VF-14 was embarked aboard USS FRANKLIN D. ROOSEVELT (CVA-42) as part of Air Wing One. (U.S. Navy)

The flight had just completed a southerly leg of their race track pattern and were headed north when the MiG calls indicated that the action was headed in their direction. The MiGs were estimated to be above the overcast (as expected) and both RIOs quickly plotted courses to place the flight in a position to intercept them. This was Bob Elliot's ninth combat mission, which made him a 'nugget', and Freeborn kept reminding him to check their six for MiGs.

Suddenly, Red Crown broadcast a MiG call that put the MiGs right where Freeborn had been warning Elliot to look...fifteen miles behind their flight. Davis broke hard left, with Freeborn following and crossing under the lead Phantom to maintain position. As he was sliding under Davis, looking up at his Phantom, Freeborn spotted the ghostly outline of an airplane beginning to break through the overcast. Within milleseconds the indistinct outline became the unmistakeable planform of first one, then two MiG-21s. The MiGs were dull silver, with no apparent markings, and both carried wing tanks.

The F-4s were in the MiGs blind spot and within seconds they were at the MiGs six o'clock position. The MiGs continued to descend slowly, at about 400 knots, apparently unaware of the Phantoms. Freeborn called; "MiGs! One o'clock high!" Davis rogered that he had them and both F-4s went to afterburner to close to minimum firing range. The Phantom pilots quickly set up their weapons systems as they closed on the MiGs. The two North Vietnamese fighters were flying the same relative formation as the Phantoms and it looked like both were going to be shot down simultaneously. Davis called; "I'll take the one on the right!" His RIO got a good lock on the MiG and he squeezed off a Sparrow. Nothing! Nothing happened! Every second in this situation was precious. The MiG controller could not help spotting the two unfriendly blips behind his fighters, and if he warned the MiG pilots, or if they happened to turn around and spot the Americans —the advantage would be lost. The MiG-21 could easily out turn the F-4 and they might get away.

Freeborn had decided not to take a chance on his 'nugget' RIO's radar skills, since they were closing to within firing range of the heat-seeking Sidewinders...a relatively simple missile that didn't require radar acquisition, tracking, or lock on. As Davis was experiencing the frustration of a dud Sparrow, Freeborn got a good annunciator tone on his Sidewinders and fired. The Sidewinder dropped off the wing pylon, squiggled around like its namesake, and guided straight to the MiG. It exploded in a brilliant flash just to the left of the MiG, which immediately began to stream either smoke or fuel. Davis had switched to HEAT when his Sparrow failed to fire and, with a good tone, fired off an AIM-9 of his own. It was a carbon copy of Freeborn's missile, failing to explode close enough to the MiG to kill it. He fired another Sidewinder, but it failed to guide, arcing off in a ballistic curve.

The MiG pilots had finally got the message that something was

VF-14's sister squadron aboard ROOSEVELT on this cruise was VF-32 Swordsmen. This Swordsmen Phantom carries TERs on the outboard wing plyons and Sidewinders on the inboard pylons as it flies a MIGCAP mission on 6 December 1966. (U.S. Navy)

The crew of this VF-92 F-4B have manned their aircraft and are ready to be towed into position for launch from USS ENTERPRISE (CVAN-65) on 4 April 1966. The Phantom carries a scoreboard of thirty-four missions on the splitter plate in the form of a small Black bomb symbol for each mission. (U.S. Navy)

not right, but instead of breaking hard to lose their attackers, they began a gentle weave, which only increased the overtake speed of the Phantoms. Davis pulled up in a high yo-yo to avoid overshooting the MiGs. Freeborn, farther back, just slowed and kept the MiGs in his sights. Before he could fire again, Davis completed his yo-yo, coming out behind the MiG that Freeborn had damaged. He was at 14,000 feet and descending behind the MiG, which was in a 45 degree banked left turn. Davis fired his third Sidewinder, which flashed out in front of the Phantom and guided straight up the MiG's tailpipe, exploding it in a huge fireball. Davis fourth and last Sidewinder, squeezed off a fraction of a second later, guided to and exploded in the fireball.

Freeborn, intent on the MiG, had not seen Davis' maneuver and was shocked to see his target draw two missile contrails and explode in front of him. "The bastard shot my MiG!", he hollered to Elliot. But the second MiG was well within range and was now trying to evade his attackers. He was in a hard, nose-up, left turn. Freeborn put his nose down, picked up speed, and pulled hard to try to cut inside the MiG's circle. His Sidewinders started to growl, indicating they were 'seeing' the MiGs heat. Freeborn squeezed the trigger to fire his second Sidewinder. Nothing happened...another dud missile. He got that sinking feeling...but squeezed again. The third Sidewinder fired off the rail and tracked straight into the MiG, disappearing momentarily into its fuselage before blowing up. The MiG exploded in another big fireball, with the cockpit area spinning out of the explosion and tumbling to the ground. Davis and Freeborn watched both MiGs impact the ground, with neither North Vietnamese pilot ejecting.

The entire action had taken less than two minutes and, as the MiGs crashed into the ground, the Phantoms turned and headed for the coast. Freeborn kept reminding Elliot to check six for more MiGs. They were low on fuel and couldn't afford much of an engagement. They rendezvoused with the tanker, refueled, and headed for CONNIE. Because they had been on the INTREPID's radio frequency during the engagement, no one on CONSTELLATION had any idea of what had happened. Freeborn's misfired Sidewinder broke loose when he trapped, skittering over the deck and falling into the Gulf of Tonkin. That brought the deck crew's attention to the fact that several other missiles on both aircraft had been fired. It didn't take long for the story to circulate among the 5,000 man crew. These kills were only the second and third MiG-21 shoot-downs for the Navy and the first for the Phantom. The story demanded telling and re-telling, both on the ship and at a news conference in Saigon the following day.

A pair of VF-92 Silver Kings' F-4Bs enroute to targets in North Vietnam carry less than a full bomb load during the much-denied (by the Johnson Administration) bomb shortage of 1966. The bombs on the outboard pylons appear to be WW II vintage 250 pound bombs. (U.S. Navy)

With flaps, hook, landing gear, and slats down, an F4B of VF-92 makes a short final for recovery aboard USS ENTERPRISE after an air strike against North Vietnam during 1966. The destroyer, in formation behind the carrier, was the search and rescue 'plane guard' destroyer. (McDonnell Aircraft)

(Above) This F-4B of VF-92 recovered at Danang after a 1967 mission from USS ENTERPRISE. Weather or possible aircraft problems were the usual reasons for diverting to shore bases and Danang served as the primary divert field for carrier-based aircraft. (via Nicholas J. Waters III)

(Right) LCDR Sitex's Phantom also suffered major damage to the starboard flap and picked up several large holes in the bottom of the wing. Even seriously damaged the Phantom was still able to bring its crew safely back from North Vietnam. (McDonnell Aircraft)

(Above) This F-4G of VF-142, piloted by LCDR Tom Sitex (who had worked at McDonnell as a Navy acceptance pilot) made an emergency landing at Danang after being damaged by an SA-2 over North Vietnam. The explosion tore off a major section of the starboard stabilator. (McDonnell Aircraft)

(Right) The Phantom had literally dozens of holes from the SAM's warhead and it was a minor miracle that the hydraulics were not hit, although all the fuselage fuel tanks were hit and leaking fuel. Two weeks later, another Phantom flown by Tom Sitex took a direct hit from a SAM. The aircraft and crew did not survive this hit. (McDonnell Aircraft)

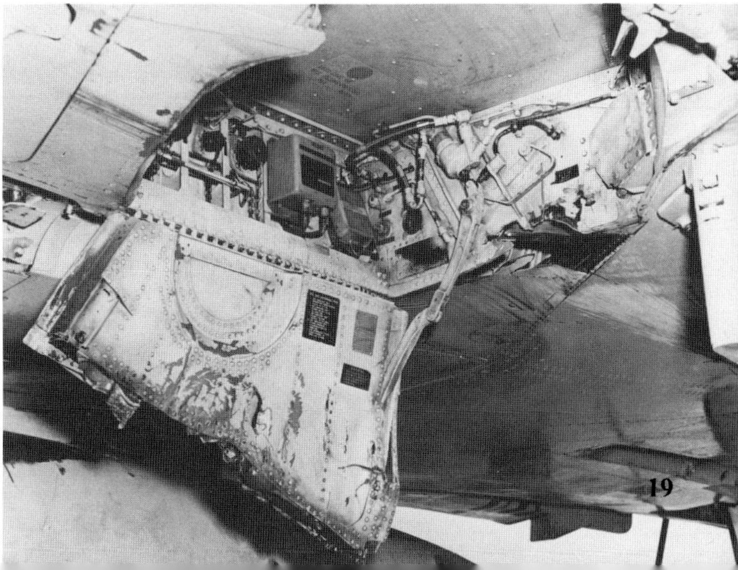

An F-4B of VF-21 is hooked to the waist catapult bridle of the number three catapult aboard USS RANGER in preparation for launch on a 13 December 1967 MIGCAP mission. The KA-3B tanker on the outboard catapult will be launched after the Phantom. (U.S. Navy)

A MIGCAP F-4B is launched from USS RANGER for a December 1967 mission against North Vietnam, while an A-7B Corsair II is prepared for launch from the inboard catapult. (U.S. Navy)

(Above) This F-4B of VF-143 Puking Dogs flies a BARCAP mission from USS CONSTELLATION on Yankee Station, 27 August 1968. The squadron nickname was derived from the posture of the Griffin squadron insignia painted on the tail. (U.S. Navy)

(Below) Armed with Mk 84 1,000 pound low drag bombs an F-4B of VF-21 heads for its target in North Vietnam during September of 1968. This configuration is unusual in that the Phantom carries no air-to-air armament or external fuel tanks. (U.S. Navy)

Tucker's First MiG Engagement

Before he made his MiG kill in August of 1972 Gene Tucker had a very memorable and frustrating MiG engagement. It happened on his first combat cruise during 1968.

On 31 March 1968 Lyndon Johnson announced his intention not to run for reelection and ordered a unilateral halt to all bombing of North Vietnam above the 19th parallel. After that, MiG engagements became increasingly rare, since the majority of MiG bases were around Hanoi, well north of the 19th parallel. That made the result of this engagement all the more frustrating. As Gene Tucker tells it:

"On 22 June 1968 I was flying a MIGCAP mission with my Radar Intercept Officer, LTJG Cosmo Salibello. I was flying wingman to then CAPT Charlie Wilson, a USAF pilot on exchange duty with our squadron. We were attached to Fighter Squadron 33 (VF-33), commanded by CDR Bill Knutson as part of Carrier Air Wing Six (CVW-6) led by CDR L. Wayne Smith. We were flying from the deck of USS AMERICA (CVA-66), commanded by CAPT D.D. Engen (who later headed the Federal Aviation Administration after he retired from the Navy). The Carrier Group Commander was RADM Jack Christianson (who later retired and became a Vice President with Grumman Aerospace Corporation).

It was mid-afternoon and we were holding 'feet wet' off the coast of North Vietnam just east of Vinh, in the vicinity of Hon Mat Island at 10,000 to 15,000 feet. Our configuration was the standard F-4J MIGCAP load, which included a centerline tank, two AIM-7E Sparrows on stations three and seven, and two AIM-9B Sidewinders on wing stations two and eight. This was the first deployment, combat or otherwise, for the F-4J with its AN/AWG-10 pulse-doppler radar. It was also the first combat deployment for USS AMERICA.

A section of MiG-17 Frescos was detected headed south and the fighter controllers passed the code word over guard frequency for all friendly aircraft to vector feet wet so there would not be any confusion or friendly versus friendly engagements. Shortly after this transmission, our section was told to vector for Blue Bandits (MiG-17s) 35-40 NM northwest of us, headed southeast. We headed due west for the first minute or so to get on their flight path prior to turning northwest.

As we coasted-in, I could see an A-7A Corsair II coming directly at us, headed towards the Gulf of Tonkin. The pilot was LT George Webb (later CO of VA-81) who, upon seeing us headed right at him, was concerned that we might mistake him for the MiGs. In those days, the J-79 engine was a bad smoker, which made the F-4J at military power easy to sight under most conditions. Webb switched his radio to guard and transmitted; "Don't shoot! F-4s, don't shoot!" Good headwork on his part, although unnecessary. We got a tally-ho on him at seven miles, on our noses. We saw the MiGs on our pulse-doppler radar and Cos, a superb radar operator, had them locked up bearing 310 degrees at 25 miles as we crossed the beach at about 3,500 feet. We turned to 310 degrees and proceeded directly at them, a track which took us right up the Son Ca River valley. We were cleared to fire at that time and were all armed up. We had elected not to jettison our centerline tanks since we had been above jettison speed from the time we received our vector to the MiGs.

CAPT Wilson had the lead until we made the turn, however, his RIO did not have radar contact, so we took the tactical lead at that time. We were in a combat spread formation with Charlie about a mile and a quarter on my right beam and stepped up 1,500 to 2,500 feet.

We closed 'straight down the pipe'. The weather was very clear; visibility was super...CAVU...and I got a tallyho at about ten miles. At seven miles I could tell that they were a section of MiG-17s. I was amazed to see that, not only were they continuing straight at me and into the envelope of my trusty forward-firing Sparrows, but that they were flying so close together that they actually looked like they had wing overlap...like the Blue Angels. The wingman had to have nearly 100 percent of his attention on his leader, he was flying such a close formation. I recall thinking that they were dumb to come straight at me, since I had a forward kill capability and they didn't (except for a minimal head-on gun shot opportunity). If they remained in that formation I could get them both with one missile (not that I intended to fire only one!). I looked through that windscreen and saw a Navy Cross! We had selected minimum afterburner at about twelve miles to kill some of our smoke and had built our speed to 550 knots.

We continued to close and were 'in range' at about six to seven miles. We had decided to wait until approaching mid-range. At about four and a half miles we were at optimum range. They were about two degrees left of my nose with a steady bearing and fire control solution as I squeezed the trigger to fire a Sparrow with all systems indicating 'up'. The 1.4 seconds between trigger squeeze and a Sparrow coming off the fuselage station is the longest 1.4 seconds in the world. I squeezed the trigger to fire the second Sparrow at about the same time I realized that

An F-4B Phantom of VF-21 and an A-7B Corsair II of VA-147 are positioned on the catapults of USS RANGER prior to a December 1967 Alpha Strike against North Vietnam. This was the first combat cruise for the A-7 Corsair II. (U.S. Navy)

The crew of a VF-33 Tarsiers F-4B Phantom mans their aircraft during carrier qualifications aboard USS AMERICA (CVA-66) during April of 1965. Even when home, the carriers and air wings were busy with refresher training, carrier qualifications, and operational readiness exercises. (U.S. Navy)

This F-4B of VF-21 armed with bombs on Triple Ejector Racks (TERs) is enroute to a target in South Vietnam from the southern carrier operating area — Dixie Station. Squadron ordnancemen have written *NO DEPOSIT, NO RETURN* on the outboard Mk 84 1,000 pound bomb. (U.S. Navy)

there was a problem with the first missile. It didn't take me long to realize that neither missile was working properly, although at the time I didn't know why. At our altitude and airspeed...low and fast...there was a moderate airframe buffet and I did not feel the missiles leave the airplane. (They had, but as I was to find out later, they had been improperly loaded. A cotter pin was inadvertently left out where the upper motor fire connector lanyard was attached to the fuselage station ejector foot. As a result, the motor fire voltage was never passed to the missiles and they were simply jettisoned when I squeezed the trigger.)

The situation had changed. Instead of the MiGs dodging my Sparrows, they now had me in their sights! I continued to close them head-on, watching for the tell-tale muzzle flashes that would show they were shooting guns. To this day, I don't know if you can tell from virtually head-on with 800 or so knots of closure, but I was sure looking! We passed within less than 50 feet of the left side of each other...'eyeball to eyeball'. Just like Randy Cunningham likes to say, "I could see their little Gomer hats and their little Gomer goggles."

I immediately started a nose-high port reversal, selecting full afterburner. In the meantime, my wingman had turned into them and as I passed the MiGs he had 90 degrees on them, with his nose on them. Unfortunately, he had a 'nugget' RIO and although his system was working, he still did not have them locked up. He called for his RIO to go 'boresight' (slave the radar antenna to the nose/gunsight) and put the pipper on the MiGs. He squeezed the trigger twice and both Sparrows fired off the fuselage stations. He had been, however, a little too quick on the trigger. His RIO had not managed to get the system into boresight quick enough and both missiles went ballistic.

At the time, I couldn't figure out why he didn't roll in on their tails, but I now believe that those MiGs turned into him and departed to the north as he overshot. I had lost sight of the MiGs as I started my reversal, but after completing about 90 degrees of turn I picked up Charlie in a left turn at my 8:30 position and four to five miles...with a MiG-17 at his 7 o'clock, about a mile away. I called the MiG to Charlie and told him to keep coming left, planning to continue my reversal and shoot the MiG off Charlie's tail. As I continued my turn, I started wondering how the MiG had gotten on his tail so fast...then realized that it could not possibly be one of the MiGs we had passed! I now felt sure there were more MiGs around than the two we had spotted first. I got nervous, overbanked to the left, and checked inside my turn. I didn't see anything there, but when I rolled back to the right to check, there was a MiG-17 at 4:30 low and a mile and a half. He was about 30 degrees nose high and pointed right at me. I estimated his speed at 350 knots and decelerating and figured he wasn't carrying Atolls...I didn't see any on him (but at a mile and a half, who can?). Many MiG-17s were loaded guns-only in those days. I decided that: (1) My MiG was not a big threat to me...he was out of range and decelerating, while I was accelerating like a speeding bullet through about 550 knots. (2) If I turned into my MiG I would have to go several turns at best to get a shot and (3) I was needed more by Charlie because of his MiG anyway. I made my decision to go for Charlie's MiG.

I reversed left, picked up Charlie and his MiG at about my 9 o'clock, about four miles and continued pulling hard down into them. They were at about 3,000 to 4,000 feet and I had peaked out at 8,000 to 10,000 feet. They had turned through another 60 degrees of turn and I was trying to figure out how to prevent a big overshoot while trying to get to the 6 o'clock of Charlie's MiG. Just then I spotted a white contrail pass over my canopy from about 7:30 to 1:30. It didn't take long to identify it as a missile and I immediately broke hard left and up into the threat. I saw a silver MiG-21 up around 20,000 feet and going the speed of heat...I estimated about 1.3 Mach or faster...in a left turn. I was down around 5,000 feet by this time and the Atoll missile had not come close to me. The MiG continued his turn and disappeared towards the north before I could get him in my sights...and with his speed and altitude advantage, he was well out of my fir-

Armed for air-to-air fighting with four AIM-9 Sidewinders and two AIM-7 Sparrow missiles, this F-4B of VF-51 returns to USS CORAL SEA after an uneventful mission over Vietnam during January of 1968. (U.S. Navy)

USS CORAL SEA (CVA-43) was one of three carriers in the MIDWAY Class (including USS MIDWAY and USS FRANKLIN D. ROOSEVELT) built in the waning days of World War II and later converted with angled decks. The MIDWAY class displaced 64,000 tons (compared to 40,000 tons for the 27 Charlie class and 90,000 tons for supercarriers). (U.S. Navy)

Navy carrier air wings flew into Naval Air Station Cubi Point in The Phillippines enroute to and from the war zone. NAS Cubi was used for maintenance, both mechanical and spiritual. This F-4B is from VF-161 off the USS CORAL SEA during 1967. (Nicholas J. Waters III)

ing envelope. I turned back to Charlie and picked him up at about two miles and 11 o'clock. He was coming right at me, headed east, and the MiG had disappeared from his tail. We passed, checked each others six o'clock, then tried to get into some kind of a tactical formation while we checked for the MiGs.

There were no MiGs in sight, so I said; "Lets get the hell out of here!" and we both turned east. I unloaded, accelerated, and headed for the Gulf. I kept descending and ended up on the deck going about 1.2 Mach...and really smoked out of there! If there were any unbroken windows or china in Vinh up to that time, there could not have been after I passed. I'm sure I had one hell of a shockwave. I knew I was fast...the canopy was too hot to touch, but I didn't realize how low I was until we crossed the 'gooseneck' of the Son Ca river east-southeast of Vinh and passed beside a small sampan with a Vietnamese fisherman standing in it. I felt like I was almost level with him. In truth, I must have been at 50 to 100 feet because I was looking up at Hon Nieu Island as I coasted out and it is only about 200 feet high. After we were well out to sea I slowed, climbed, and joined up with Charlie for the return to the carrier.

In retrospect, although the controllers only saw one section of MiGs, there was a second section three to five miles in trail at low altitude, and that MiG-21 sitting way up there high over the fight. We should have seen the second section sooner, but we got so engrossed with the lead section that we never considered the possibility of a set-up. The North Vietnamese were developing this ambush tactic and used it a lot after that. Once we caught on to it, we decided to have the wingman continue through a MiG section, looking for the trailers with his radar, while the leader went after the lead section. In actual practice though, when most fighter pilots saw any MiG, they went after it...the old "A bird in the hand" philosophy.

In this engagement, the second section of MiGs were too far behind. If they had missiles, they never got into the firing envelope for them, although Charlie's MiG was sure nibbling at it! If they didn't have missiles, they weren't even close to a shot. The MiG-21 pilot just flat blew it. He must have been inexperienced and scared because he surely could have had me for lunch, because I had no idea he was there. All he had to do was point his nose down at me as I was pitching back on the first MiG section and close me to get into the envelope. I was fortunate that he was a 'plumber', because we all lived to fly and fight another day...and night.

A section of F-4B Phantoms of VF-11 Red Rippers fly over the Northern Tonkin Gulf during a 1967 Barrier Combat Air Patrol (BARCAP) mission. VF-11 was part of Air Group Seventeen aboard USS FORRESTAL (CVA-59). (U.S. Navy via Nicholas J. Waters III)

USS ENTERPRISE (CVAN-65) was the first nuclear-powered carrier and the only nuclear carrier to participate in the Vietnam War. She was commissioned on 27 October 1961 and displaced 89,600 tons. The supply ship alongside ENTERPRISE is USS SHASTA (AE-6). (U.S. Navy)

ADMIRAL JOHN DISHER

....has spent almost an entire Naval Aviation career in fighters. His experiences with the F-4 came in the middle of his flying career and makes an interesting comparison between the fighters that came before the Phantom and those that have followed.

"I was in VF-33, which was a part of Carrier Air Group 6, aboard USS ENTERPRISE (CVAN-65). I had started out flying Grumman F-11s in VF-33, making one cruise in the Tiger before transitioning to an early model of the LTV F-8 Crusader, still in VF-33. We made one cruise aboard the 27 Charlie Class carrier USS INTREPID (CVA-11) with F-8s, then the composition of the air group was changed. Our sister squadron, VF-74, was scheduled to become an all-weather fighter squadron. VF-74 was the first fleet squadron to get the F-4B Phantom II. VF-102, the second East Coast squadron to get the F-4, was also in the air group. We re-equipped with brand-new F8U-2NE (F-8E) Crusaders. We went aboard USS ENTERPRISE for a brief Mediterranean cruise. It is the only time I had been in the Med during the summer and it was great. We returned to Norfolk and were not scheduled to deploy again for almost a year.

Our next deployment was to have been with ENTERPRISE for an around-the-world-cruise during 1963...but the Cuban Missile Crisis intervened. We deployed to operate in the Caribbean from early October of 1962 until just before Christmas. During this cruise we became very serious about tactics, developing a number of joint F-4/F-8 missions. I flew several missions on the wing of the F-4, particularly at night, where the Phantom's more powerful radar and two man crew made for more effective intercepts. At that time the Phantom was operating strictly as an interceptor, engaging in very little air combat maneuvering (ACM). The F-8 was the primary Navy dogfighter.

My first hands-on experience with the F-4 came after I had attended the British test pilot school at Farnborough, England. I returned from England to an assignment with VX-4, at NAS Point Mugu, California. VX-4 is the operational testing squadron which develops fighter tactics and evaluates, in an operational environment, the weapons and weapons systems of the aircraft. I spent two years with VX-4, flying the F-4. The last year was spent in evaluating the AIM-7 Sparrow and AIM-9 Sidewinder in an air combat maneuvering environment. This testing was in response to reports we were receiving from Southeast Asia. Neither one of the missiles had been designed for the kind of dogfighting that was taking place over North Vietnam between F-4s and MIG-17s (and later MiG-21s).

One of the more exciting phases of that project was an intense three week period in which I was given twenty-two drone aircraft and all the missiles I could shoot. I was to come up with a quick evaluation of the AIM-9B and AIM-9C Sidewinders and AIM-7D Sparrow in an ACM environment, defining the limitations of each missile. Afterward I would recommend changes that could be made quickly, changes which would make them better air-to-air weapons. At the same time there was another project group working to develop more effective tactics.

We made several recommendations for changes to the missiles, particularly in the fusing. The fusing changes could be made immediately, however, the guidance changes we recommended would take time to develop. Both missiles had been designed for use against bombers and were fused to allow the missile to penetrate the target before going off. Against a fast, maneuvering target, the chances for penetration are not real good and we suggested that the experts at China Lake change to a proximity fuse which would set off the warhead when it got close enough to do damage to the more vulnerable fighter sized target.

I made two combat cruises in the Phantom, both with VF-96, in Air Wing Nine aboard ENTERPRISE. Both cruises were during periods in which bombing restrictions were in force, limiting our raids against North Vietnam to below the 17th parallel. While we regularly flew MIGCAP missions off the coast of Haiphong, there was very little action. Most of the strike missions were flown into South Vietnam and Laos.

The first cruise started in an interesting manner. It was February of 1968 and the TET Offensive had just begun. We were sortied out of Sasebo, Japan enroute to Subic Bay to pick up our combat load of weapons when word came that the North Koreans had captured the USS PUEBLO. We were directed up into the Sea of Japan, off the coast of Korea. The only way we could be supplied by air and it took what seemed like days of around-the-clock airlifts of Grumman C-2s to fly all our stuff aboard. You can't operate in the Sea of Japan in February without an exposure suit. If you were shot down or crashed, you wouldn't survive more than a few minutes in that near-freezing water. Since we had been headed for the tropical Gulf of Tonkin, only two squadrons had packed their exposure suits. Until ade-

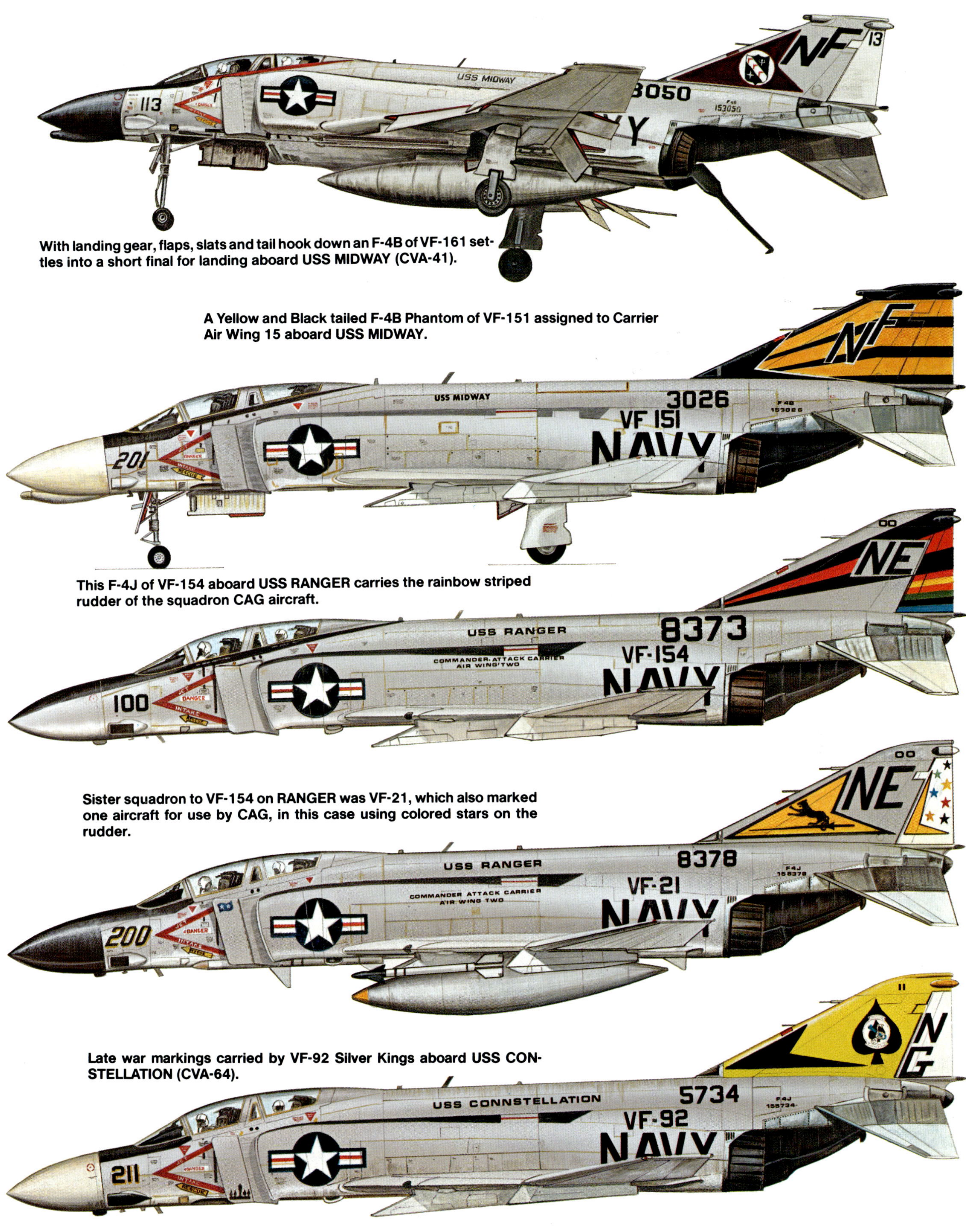

With landing gear, flaps, slats and tail hook down an F-4B of VF-161 settles into a short final for landing aboard USS MIDWAY (CVA-41).

A Yellow and Black tailed F-4B Phantom of VF-151 assigned to Carrier Air Wing 15 aboard USS MIDWAY.

This F-4J of VF-154 aboard USS RANGER carries the rainbow striped rudder of the squadron CAG aircraft.

Sister squadron to VF-154 on RANGER was VF-21, which also marked one aircraft for use by CAG, in this case using colored stars on the rudder.

Late war markings carried by VF-92 Silver Kings aboard USS CONSTELLATION (CVA-64).

An F-4J of VF-92 makes a barrier landing aboard USS AMERICA (CVA-66) while on Yankee Station in the Gulf of Tonkin, 21 July 1970. Although the Phantom's tailhook is extended, the deck arresting wires do not appear to have been rigged. (U.S. Navy)

quate supplies of the suits were flown aboard, we had to share the use of survival suits. Our squadron got enough suits for four crews and they were in constant use. A crew would land, climb out of their hot, sweaty, suits and you would have to pull it on and brief for the next flight! We did that for three or four days before enough suits could be flown out to the ship to outfit everyone with their own...then you only had to smell your own sweat when you suited up.

We finally headed for Vietnam, arriving on Dixie Station off the coast of South Vietnam in late February. Typically, the carrier would spend four or five days on Dixie Station, operating in the relatively benign environment of South Vietnam, before heading for Yankee Station, off the coast of North Vietnam. During the work-up period on Dixie Station we had a chance to work out the kinks, respond to the FAC, drop live ordnance...and get mentally prepared for the much tougher arena over the North. We got to Yankee Station just prior to the bombing halt above the 19th parallel and were able to run a couple of strikes into the Haiphong area and one almost to the Chinese border. The weather was generally pretty poor though and we didn't fly many missions before the bombing halt forced us to limit our operations to Route Packages Two and Three. Route Package One, which was just above the Demilitarized Zone (DMZ) was almost exclusively Air Force territory.

The catapult crewman checks the bridle tension on an F-4B of VF-161 as the Phantom is prepared for launch from USS CORAL SEA on 20 December 1969. At this stage of the war, bombing missions were not being flown over North Vietnam, although Laos and South Vietnam got plenty of attention. (U.S. Navy)

The F-4s were being operated exclusively as bombers, although we always went off with two Sidewinders and two Sparrows. Usually the Sparrows were carried in the aft missile wells. The one exception to this was when we flew in the three drop tank configuration with Mark 82 bombs on the inboard wing stations. This configuration created an aft center of gravity (CG) situation that forced us to move the Sparrows to the forward missile wells. Normally, when you took a cat shot in the F-4, you held the stick about half way back, which rotated the nose to a flying attitude as soon as you cleared the catapult. When we started flying missions into Laos, we had to fly south to the DMZ, cross South Vietnam into Laos, then head some distance north. When we got there we were forced to hold because of the traffic jams of fighters caused by diverting all the strikes which would have gone into North Vietnam. The FACs would have us stacked in holding patterns and this required lots of gas, hence the three tank configuration.

In the three tank configuration, the CG is moved well aft and when you cleared the catapult, you got an immediate pitch-up. You actually had to apply forward stick to prevent a stall. This made for some very exciting night catapult shots. At night, on the water, there is very little, if any, natural horizon and if you don't transition to the gages fast enough, or if you don't anticipate that pitch-up, you could get into the stall/buffet/wing rock regime very fast. A couple of our younger pilots provided some fairly interesting moments when this happened. They finally had to hit the master panic button, which cleaned everything off the bottom of the aircraft, in order to save it. During this period, the flying around the ship was more exciting than combat, which often consisted of blind delivery of bombs through clouds, using radar offsets from a ground station. Later, the North Vietnamese moved a number of SAM radars and SA-2s into southern North Vietnam and it got more exciting. They also began introducing the hand-held SA-7 Strella heat-seeking SAM to their ground troops, but we didn't see enough of them to constitute a real threat until 1972. The SA-7 was not much of a threat to an F-4 unless you made multiple runs on the same target, giving them a chance to anticipate your pattern. That's exactly how Harley Hall, former leader of the Blue Angels, got bagged.

Our normal line period was thirty days, during which we would fly five days, take one day off, then fly again for five days. In between line periods, we would have inport periods at places like Hong Kong or Singapore. There were normally three carriers involved, with two on line and one in port.

At the end of the first combat cruise, we took our newly overhauled F-4Bs down to Cubi Point, in the Philippines. At Cubi we washed them, did all the anti-corrosion work, then flew them to Chu Lai, South Vietnam. At Chu Lai we exchanged them for some very worn-out Marine Phantoms which had been in-country for a very long time. I was the squadron assistant maintenance officer and had to sign off the yellow sheets when we turned our aircraft over. I was in the last flight to arrive at Chu Lai and as I signed off on my aircraft's yellow sheet, I looked up to see the first of our F-4s taking off with a load of bombs on its first mission for the Marines. They had not wasted any time in turning those aircraft around! Their maintenance officer slapped me on the back and said; "Boy, are we glad to see you guys! These things look like they just came off the showroom floor!" Well, they were pretty old F-4Bs, but they had just made the one cruise after being overhauled and we had washed them before delivering them to the Marines. Compared to what they had been flying, I guess they did look pretty good.

We had to spend the night at Chu Lai amidst the mosquitoes, heat, and rocket attacks. We were real anxious to get out of there in the morning and thankful that we could operate from a ship. The plane captain helped me strap in and, as he scooted my helmet across the top of the ejection seat, a handful of sand filtered down the back of my flight suit. The cockpit was full of sand! I was the last guy to take off and, of the ten aircraft, mine was the only one with a good radar. We were all strung out, try-

ing to get joined up, as we headed across the South China Sea towards the Philippines. When we arrived, four of the ten had immediate action emergencies, ranging from hydraulic to generator failures. We cleaned them up, hoisted them aboard ship, and sailed for CONUS. We had the understanding that we were going to turn these wrecks into the overhaul facility as soon as we arrived. We were supposed to get brand-new F-4Js, but production delays forced us to keep those Marine F-4s for four months. They provided some exciting moments. One of them was christened 'The Flying Banana' because every time you took a cat shot, you got an uncommanded rudder deflection which threw the aircraft into a skid, which bled off airspeed at a very critical time. We were never able to find the cause of the problem and eventually just grounded the aircraft.

During my second combat cruise the ENTERPRISE suffered a tremendous fire off the coast of Hawaii. We were in the middle of our Operational Readiness Exercise (ORE), which was the final certification that we were combat-ready. I had just started to brief the next flight in Ready Room One (forward) when the first bombs went off aft. One of the jet starting unit tractors had been parked with its exhaust next to the warheads on a Zuni rocket pod. The hot exhaust cooked off the Zuni warheads and when they exploded, they ruptured the aircraft's fuel tanks which started an immediate fire on the deck. The fire in turn began to cook off the Mk 82 bombs we had loaded on the aircraft. We have closed-circuit television monitors in the ready rooms so that we can observe cat shots and landings. I saw the first bomb flash on one of these and thought; "Geez, it's FORRESTAL all over again!" (FORRESTAL had suffered the same kind of accident a year and a half earlier.) The difference between this fire and the FORRESTAL fire was that the crew of ENTERPRISE never stopped fighting the fire until it was out. There was a period during the FORRESTAL fire that they had stopped fighting the fire.

The fire took three hours to extinguish and cost the lives of twenty-eight crewmen. Among the dead were the crew of the aircraft where the fire started. The RIO was just blown away, while the pilot was ejected when the heat of the fire cooked off his ejection seat. He was recovered and lived for about two weeks before finally succumbing to his injuries. Our Ordnance Officer had been under that aircraft, and all we ever found of him was his wallet. We lost several plane captains and ground crewmen, but the majority of casualties were among the fire-fighters. Fifteen aircraft were destroyed and the repairs to the ship, which were done in Hawaii, cost 56 million dollars. While the repairs were being made, the F-4 squadrons operated out of MCAS Kaneohe Bay, with the Marines. The fire had started among our squadron aircraft and we had lost almost half of our aircraft, so it took us a while to get the replacements and get up to speed. We had been equipped with brand-new F-4Js and I can remember the feeling of pride on the morning we reported all thirteen aircraft 'up', ready to go — with good radars and all systems operational.

A division of F-4Js from VF-154 Black Knights in formation over the South China Sea during January of 1970. Only the rear Phantom carries the squadron insignia, a Black Knight's helmet, on the fuselage side. VF-154 was embarked aboard USS RANGER (CVA-61). (U.S. Navy)

We finally arrived on Yankee Station in October. The weather was pretty bad and we did a lot of blind bombing on the wing of Loran or radar equipped bombers. We also did a lot of work in Laos and the ship was operating south of Yankee Station in order to shorten the distance we had to fly. That made for some pretty long MIGCAP missions north, since we still maintained the CAP station off of Haiphong...just in case the North Vietnamese decided to try to attack the ship (they never did). The following April, we were diverted to the Sea of Japan again. The North Koreans had shot down a Lockheed EC-121 Warning Star radar surveillance aircraft, killing all thirty-one on board. Our show of force lasted less than a month.

After that cruise, I attended the Naval Warfare College, then was assigned as Executive Officer of VX-4, in preparation for taking over as Commanding Officer. The changes in the F-4 weapons and systems was dramatic. The radar had been improved and we were beginning to get dogfighting missiles. Tactics had been changed too and we were doing a lot of ACM. It was during this period that we added the first rear-view mirrors to the top of the rear cockpit canopy frame, so that the RIO would have better view of the aircraft's six o'clock position. It was an idea we borrowed from the Israelis and, although Naval Air Systems Command wanted to perform extensive testing before installing the mirrors, we felt the Israelis had proven that it was good idea which would not degrade the performance or safety of the aircraft ...so we just installed them.

Armed with rocket pods on the outboard wing plyons, a flight of F-4Bs of VF-111 Sundowners, off USS CORAL SEA head inland enroute to their targets in South Vietnam during November of 1971. (U.S. Navy)

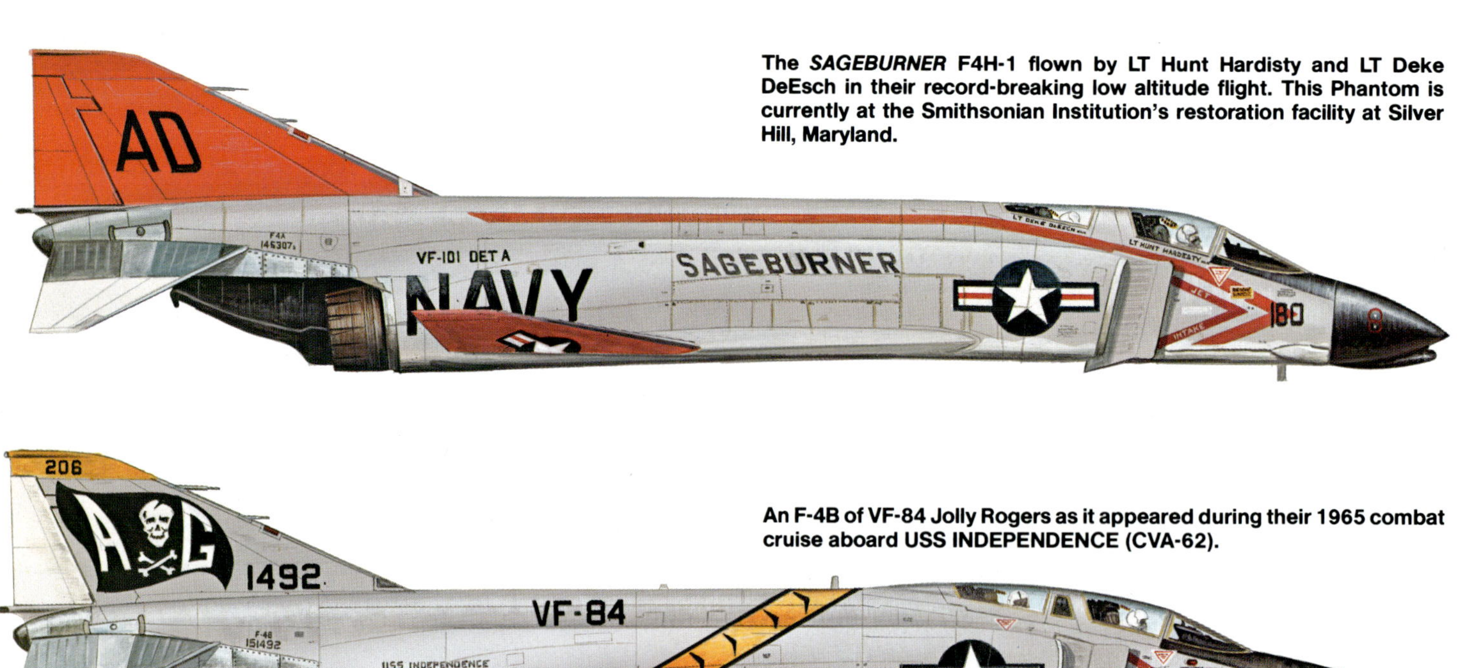

The *SAGEBURNER* F4H-1 flown by LT Hunt Hardisty and LT Deke DeEsch in their record-breaking low altitude flight. This Phantom is currently at the Smithsonian Institution's restoration facility at Silver Hill, Maryland.

An F-4B of VF-84 Jolly Rogers as it appeared during their 1965 combat cruise aboard USS INDEPENDENCE (CVA-62).

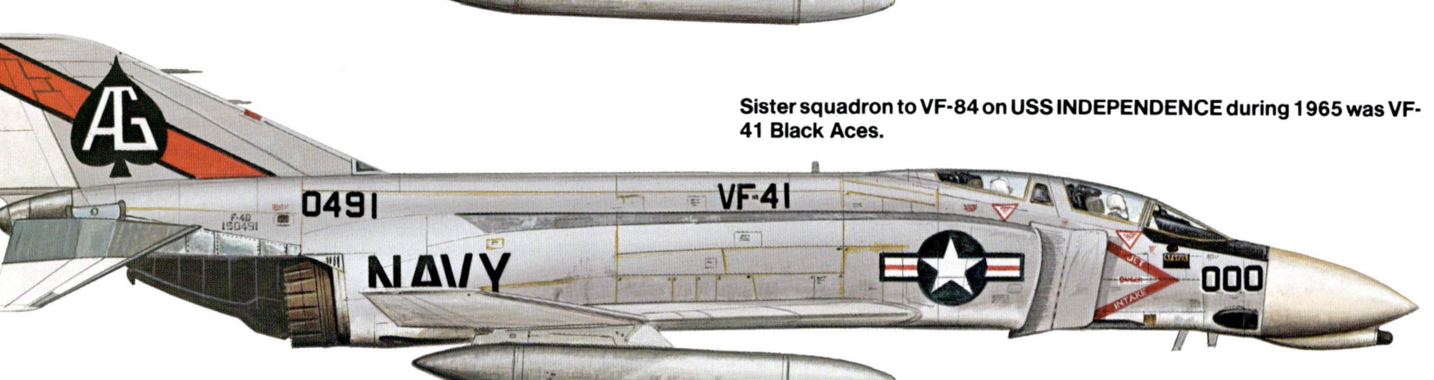

Sister squadron to VF-84 on USS INDEPENDENCE during 1965 was VF-41 Black Aces.

The sixth production Phantom is directed to the bow catapults aboard USS INDEPENDENCE (CVA-62) during carrier suitability trials held in April of 1960. (McDonnell Aircraft)

An F-4B Phantom of VF-161 lights the afterburners just prior to launch from USS CORAL SEA (CVA-43) for a mission against North Vietnam during 1968. (Nicholas J. Waters III)

An F-4B of VF-143 The 'world famous Puking Dogs' armed with Sidewinders and Sparrows, as it appeared during their 1968 combat cruise aboard USS CONSTELLATION (CVA-64).

Phantom pilots outfitted with Nomex flight suit, harness, survival vest, and anti-G suit.

VF-213 Black Lions, aboard USS KITTY HAWK (CVA-63) tested tactical camouflage during 1966. The water based Dark Green camouflage proved to be ineffective and unnecessary, since the major threat over Vietnam was from ground-based anti-aircraft fire. (McDonnell Aircraft via Robert N. Pukala)

An F-4B of VF-213 drops its load of Mk 82 low drag bombs under radar direction. These missions were flown against area targets, using radar offsets, either from ground stations or from an aircraft with ground mapping radar. (U.S. Navy via RADM James Flatley)

In late 1971 I joined Air Wing Nine, once again flying F-4Bs, this time with VF-151. We were scheduled to deploy to the Western Pacific (WESTPAC) in June of 1972 aboard USS MIDWAY (CVA-41). The Spring 1972 North Vietnamese Offensive, however, resulted in our deploying three months early. I can recall vividly how we got the word. We had been out doing night Carrier Qualifications with our new pilots. It was a Thursday night and all of a sudden we turned around and started steaming for San Francisco at thirty knots. We knew then that something was up! We arrived at Alameda the next morning and were given the word that we would sail for WESTPAC on Monday morning. In addition to seven or eight new 'Nugget' pilots, who had just arrived from the RAG, we had three aircraft in pieces at Miramar, undergoing progressive overhaul. They got the word to put them together on Thursday at midnight, turned to, and got them flying by Friday afternoon. We flew down to Miramar on Friday, packed all of our personal gear and returned to Alameda on Saturday to load the aircraft and all of our gear aboard ship. Our wives came up on Saturday too and we had a last fling in San Francisco before departing Monday.

We steamed for twenty-one days, straight to the Gulf of Tonkin. After a few days of operating in the South, we headed north for what would be a three Alpha Strike per day schedule. We operated like that up until September, when there was a brief hiatus, followed by more intense bombing of the North. In October things slowed down for peace negotiations, but after the elections the North Vietnamese started stalling again and things really got hot around Christmas. Our A-6s were tasked to provide diversionary raids while the B-52s hit Hanoi. We flew the MIGCAP missions.

My most memorable mission occurred during this period. It was an Alpha Strike that was tasked with knocking down a bridge in downtown Haiphong. I was leading the last division of aircraft. CAG was leading the first division with F-4s and there were A-7s and A-6s sandwiched in between. We also had Iron Hand (SAM suppression) support, ECM, and tankers. As soon as we pointed toward land, twenty-five miles from the coast, we were illuminated by SAM radars and they started launching on us! Our flight route would take us in about fifteen miles south of Haiphong, until we were twenty-five miles inland, then we turned directly north before heading for the target. The plan was to provide us with a minimum of overland exposure after we had released our bombs. They had us under attack for better than thirty miles and, as we maneuvered to defeat the SAMs, the flight integrity began to break down. A division of A-7s, which was two flights ahead of me, got confused and when the time came to turn right and head for the target, they turned left! The division in front of me was A-6s and they began to climb to their roll-in point, all the time getting slower, as they waited for the division of A-7s to call that they were in on the target.

The A-6 division leader had not seen the A-7s turn left and didn't realize that they were now behind us. Normally, we would roll in at about 11,000 or 12,000 feet, keeping our speed up to at least 400 knots in the climb preceding roll-in. The A-6s got to 15,000 feet...still no call and we were getting real slow...somewhere around 250 knots, which is really a marginal maneuvering speed for a loaded F-4. We began to draw AAA fire and it was fairly heavy and accurate. The A-6 leader was a guy named 'Hoagy' Carmichael and I can remember hollering at him over the radio; "Dammit Hoagy, the A-7s aren't anywhere near...roll in! Roll in, so we can get the hell outta here!" We got to 17,000

This F-4B of VF-114 off USS KITTY HAWK (CVA-63), is enroute to targets in North Vietnam on 19 April 1967. The F-4 is loaded with twelve Mk 82 500 pound Snakeye retarded bombs. Snakeye bombs could be released from much lower altitudes than conventional bombs. (U.S. Navy)

Trailing a plume of hot jet exhaust, an F-4B of VF-142 launches from the waist catapult of USS CONSTELLATION while steaming in the Gulf of Tonkin on 24 February 1970. (U.S. Navy)

feet before rolling in and ended up using about a 75 degree dive, which felt like you were going straight down! All of our release parameters had been figured for a much shallower dive angle, so we weren't sure where in the hell our bombs were going to land. I was talking to my RIO, asking him if he had any idea on what the bombsight settings and release point were. He didn't, but I figured I would release about 9,500 feet. I pickled, rolled off, looked back, and was amazed to see both my bombs and the bombs of my wingman land right on the bridge! I didn't stick around to watch the rest of the bombs land, since we were now down to 5,000 feet and really getting hosed down by AAA. There were over twenty-five SAMs fired at us on that mission — without result. I don't think we even had an aircraft hit on that mission.

Our sister squadron on MIDWAY was VF-161. They got six MiGs on that cruise and we never even saw one. Our missions were bombing, TARCAP, and BARCAP. It was a very long and exciting cruise, lasting eleven months. We were now much better prepared to fight the war in a sophisticated defense environment. We had established 'Top Gun', were getting ACM training, and we had a much better ECM suite for protection against radar directed guns and missiles.

USS KITTY HAWK (CVA-63) was commissioned in May of 1961 and was the first carrier to be equipped with Terrier surface to air missiles for air defense. KITTY HAWK displaced 80,800 tons and was involved in the Vietnam War from 1966 to 1973. (U.S. Navy via RADM James Flatley)

The Phantom was one of the best aircraft in the fleet for operating around the ship. It was very stable on the glideslope and had plenty of power when you needed it. The one big disadvantage was the rate at which those J-79 engines burned fuel. In the early F-4s, we had a very limited max landing weight, which made it pretty important that you get aboard on your first try. That was improved significantly in the F-4J. The catapult shot did require some technique. It took a few cat shots before you discovered the ideal stick position so that you didn't over-rotate and approach a stall, or under-rotate and start to settle. But it was much better than the F-8 Crusader, which was very unstable in speed control on the glideslope. The F-11 Tiger was a very good aircraft, but it didn't carry much fuel. The F-14 Tomcat, with its wings swept forward, is more sensitive in line-up for coming aboard. All things considered, I would say that the F-4 was the best aircraft for operating aboard a carrier."

F-4Bs of VF-142 and VF-143 from USS CONSTELLATION (CVA-64) drop their bombs on command while flying above a solid undercast over South Vietnam. The command to drop would be relayed from either a ground station or airborne command aircraft. (Tailhook Photo Service)

LT Winston 'Mad Dog' Copeland of VF-51 flew this F-4B from the deck of USS CORAL SEA (CVA-43) on his MiG-killing mission of 11 June 1972. LT Copeland shot down a MiG-17 with an AIM-9 Sidewinder air-to-air missile.

USS CORAL SEA
9457
NL
13
VF-51
NAVY
LOU DRENDEL

(Above) Members of the 'Purple Gang' refuel an F-4S Phantom on the deck of USS KITTY HAWK. The 'Purple Gang' got their nickname from the Purple (indicating fuels) flight deck jerseys worn by the fuel crews aboard a carrier. (U.S. Navy)

(Above) A Grumman KA-6D Intruder tanker of VA-165 refuels an F-4J of VF-92 high over the Gulf of Tonkin on 7 November 1971. Both aircraft are from the USS CONSTELLATION (CVA-64). (U.S. Navy)

(Below) An F-4J of VF-92 assigned to USS CONSTELLATION waits while his wingman takes on fuel from a Douglas EKA-3B Skywarrier tanker while on a BARCAP mission over the northern Gulf of Tonkin. (Tailhook Photo Service)

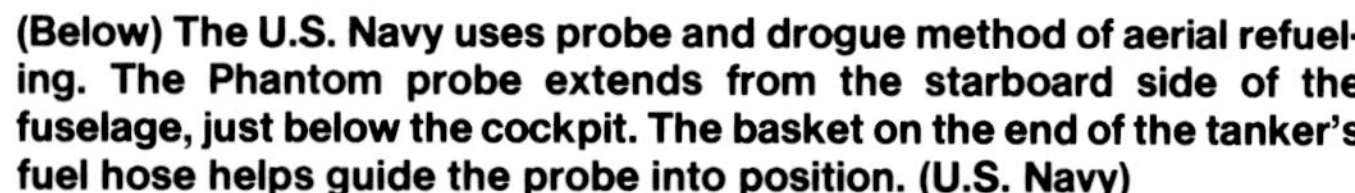

(Below) The U.S. Navy uses probe and drogue method of aerial refueling. The Phantom probe extends from the starboard side of the fuselage, just below the cockpit. The basket on the end of the tanker's fuel hose helps guide the probe into position. (U.S. Navy)

One of the primary fighter missions performed by the F-4 was escort of the RA-5C Vigilante reconnaissance aircraft over North Vietnam. The Phantom is from VF-213, while the Vigilante is from 'Heavy Eleven' (RVAH-11), both assigned to USS KITTY HAWK (CVA-63). (U.S. Navy via RADM James Flatley)

Rear Admiral James H. Flatley III

...comes from one of the most famous families in United States Naval Aviation. His father was an ace in the Second World War and Operations Officer for ADM Marc Mitscher. Two of his sons are Naval Aviators, flying F-14s and F-18s and one of his daughters is attending the Naval Academy.

After graduation from Annapolis, Jim Flatley reported to NAS Pensacola for flight training and was designated a Naval Aviator in October of 1957. His first operational squadron was VF-33 stationed at NAS Oceana flying the Grumman F-11A Tiger. He made three Med cruises aboard USS INTREPID, the last flying Vought F-8 Crusaders, before receiving orders to the Naval Test Pilots School. He graduated from USNTPS in October of 1962 and was assigned to the Carrier Suitability Branch of the Flight Test Center at NAS Patuxent River, Maryland. While at Pax River, he participated in the development and evaluation of the RA-5C Vigilante, the French variant of the F-8 Crusader and the Automatic Carrier Landing System. He also conducted evaluations of the A-3, A-4, A-5, A-6, E-2, and S-2/C-1/E-1 series of aircraft. One of his most challenging and unusual assignments was determining the carrier suitability of the C-130 Hercules.

A two year tour as LSO for Carrier Air Wing Three (CVW-3) aboard USS SARATOGA, followed Pax River. He then reported to VF-213 aboard USS KITTY HAWK (CVA-63) in 1967, first as Safety Officer than as Maintenance Officer. He made two combat deployments to WESTPAC aboard KITTY HAWK, making his 1,000th arrested landing during the second deployment, becoming the fifth Naval Aviator to reach this milestone.

In August of 1969 he attended the Air Force Command and Staff College at Maxwell AFB, Alabama. He followed that tour with a Masters Degree in Business Administration at Auburn University. After a brief stint with Commander Fleet Air Norfolk Staff, he reported to VF-31 in May of 1971 as Executive Officer. He assumed command of VF-31 on 26 May 1972 during his third combat cruise, at the height of Linebacker I operations. On that cruise, he flew his 350th combat mission. I interviewed him in 1987, after his retirement from the Navy. His recollections of his experiences were still fresh and as the most experienced Naval Aviator of his generation, (he holds the record for arrested landings at 1,607) they are particularly interesting.

My first two combat cruises were with VF-213, on USS KITTY HAWK in 1968-69. On the first combat cruise, the KITTY HAWK became the first carrier to win the Presidential Unit Citation for spending ninety consecutive days on the line. That is a pittance in this day and age, but back then it was considered remarkable. My squadron did not lose a single aircraft in any of the three combat cruises, while our sister squadrons (VF-114 on KITTY HAWK and VF-103 on SARATOGA) lost seven crews and aircraft on each cruise. Of those seven losses, probably one was in pre-combat operations, while four of the remaining six were operational losses in the Gulf of Tonkin. Only two were as a result of enemy action. That was a little worse than the fleet average, but not much ...over half our losses during the war were operational losses ... accidents around the boat, running out of fuel, mid-airs, and so forth.

On the first combat launch of my first combat cruise, Lenny Leigh, who had served with me in F-11s, was lost. We launched into a thousand foot overcast, but when we got to the beach, we saw that the weather was too bad to bomb. We all turned around and came back to the ship, except Lenny. Lenny tried to go in under the overcast, then pulled up into the goo to loft his bombs. He didn't recover. I loved that guy, but it seemed that we were continually doing dumb things like that throughout the war. I attribute just about every one of those twenty-one losses to squadron leadership... lack of discipline. I was safety officer on my first cruise, maintenance officer on my second, and CO on my third. In spite of what I considered inadequate training time during the work-up period, we came back with everyone. We took some hits in our aircraft ...one of VF-103's guys even fired a missile at one of our aircraft...but we all survived. (In the case of the accidental missile shoot, the VF-31 pilot had better situational awareness. It was a TARCAP mission and he saw the other Phantom shoot. He was able to turn 180 degrees quickly enough to prevent the Sidewinder from obtaining a heat source and locking on.)

The weather was terrible on those first two cruises. I can't tell you how many times we had to turn around and return because of bad weather over the target. The third combat cruise was more satisfying. President Nixon had upped the ante and the rules of engagement were a lot different in 1972 than they had been in 1968, particularly in Linebacker II, when the B-52s bombed Hanoi. I flew MIGCAP on some of those missions and they were impressive. Another thing that made my cruises interesting and somewhat unique, I think, was that the F-4 guys got to lead strikes. On some boats, only the attack squadron leaders led strikes. On KITTY HAWK and SARATOGA, we rotated, so that out of a hundred strikes, I got to lead seven. I even led the strike that re-mined Haiphong Harbor using A-6s and F-4s.

An F-4J of VF-114 Aardvarks aboard USS KITTY HAWK (CVA-63) during 1972. VF-114 was credited with two MiG-21s during this cruise, both shot down on 6 May 1972.

(Above) One of the most colorful Navy Phantom schemes was carried into combat by the F-4Bs of VF-51 Screaming Eagles. The rainbow tail on the eagle and '00' side number mark this Phantom as the squadron's CAG aircraft. (Duane Kasulka via Charles Howes)

(Below) NH 100, an F-4J of VF-213 Black Lions sits on the ramp with the refueling probe extended and a travel pod mounted on the inboard wing pylon. (Charles Howes)

During his MiG engagement of 22 June 1968, Gene Tucker passed a pair of North Vietnamese Air Force MiG-17 Fresco Cs almost head-on while the MiG-17s were flying in close formation.

AC 101, the MiG-killing F-4J Phantom flown by CDR Sam Flynn of VF-31 on his MiG-killing mission of 21 June 1972. (Charles Howes)

LT Gary Weigand of VF-111 flew this F-4B on his MiG-killing mission. (Duane Kasulka via Charles Howes)

Armed with a full bag of four AIM-9 Sidewinders and four AIM-7 Sparrows, this F-4B of VF-143 is plugged into the refueling receptacle of a KA-3B Skywarrior tanker over the Gulf of Tonkin during 1968. (Jim Hurley)

An F-4B of VF-114, configured with Multiple Ejector Racks (MERs) on the outboard pylons, returns to USS KITTY HAWK after a 20 April 1967 Alpha Strike against the Haiphong Thermal Power Plant. (U.S. Navy)

The most memorable missions are the ones in which you accomplish your objective and there is no doubt of it. The one that stands out in my mind is a strike that I led. It was a thirty-three aircraft Alpha Strike against a very concentrated shipyard on the Red River. The weather was really bad and even though CAG Deke Bordone was on the mission, flying an A-6 with much better navagational equipment, I was leading and it was up to me to find the target. The weather was a broken undercast, which thickened as we approached the target area. Just to spice things up, we began getting MiG calls from Red Crown, although the MiGs never showed up. The tops of the clouds were about 10,000 feet, with the bottoms at 2,000 feet. We were skimming the tops, straining to see checkpoints through holes in the clouds. The holes were becoming fewer and fewer and just when I thought we would have to turn back... there was the target in the middle of a large hole in the clouds. That was some sight and seeing thirty-three aircraft dive through that hole was some thing to see as well. The bombing parameters were really squeezed because of the weather... you really didn't want to go lower than a couple of thousand feet on your drop because of the difficulty in pulling out of your dive. As we pulled off target, everyone turned a different direction before joining up, in twos and threes, for the trip back to the ship. Not only did we find the target, we absolutely destroyed it. To cap the mission we got good Bomb Damage Assessment (BDA) photos from the recce bird.

I was on twenty or so Alpha Strikes (strikes in which thirty plus aircraft conduct a coordinated attack on a particular target) and we lost only one aircraft to the enemy. It was a SAM. I was out to the side of the gaggle of bombers, flying TARCAP, and didn't see the SAM that connected, although there were about seven of them in the air at once. The bomber gaggle just wasn't jinking as vigorously as it should have. The pilot ejected and we heard later that the North Vietnamese had killed him while still in his parachute, before he ever hit the ground.

Of course, there were other things that could get you too. During my third combat cruise, we had a rash of aileron actuator failings in the Phantom. If the actuator broke in just the right place, you lost control and had to eject. There didn't seem to be any pattern to these and maintenance was not a factor, since you could not even see the actuator in question. The fact that my squadron did not lose a single aircraft, while our sister squadron did, was just luck. Eventually all the actuators had to be replaced.

In over 4,500 hours of flying fighters or in the dangerous and demanding job of testing aircraft, Flatley never had a serious emergency. This is not necessarily a testiment to luck or exceptional maintenance, but rather aeronatutical skill, situational awareness, and self discipline in planning every flight. The rules were; follow every checklist and never, never panic. There is an old saying that goes, "There are old aviators and there are bold aviators, but there are no old, bold aviators." This is mostly true, but there are exceptions to every rule, pilots who are so at home in the sky, so attuned to their aircraft that they have a seemingly magical sixth sense in the seat of their pants. They are able to defy the law of averages. Jim Flatley is one of the exceptional aviators whose skill and leadership are responsible for success inspite of the most difficult conditions. At the height of the Linebacker I operations against North Vietnam, when the future of South Vietnam depended on the effective use of American airpower, Flatley led an Alpha Strike against one of the best defended and lucrative targets in North Vietnam. The official summary of that action reads as follows:

Phu Ly Railroad and Highway Bridges, Transshipment Point, and Heavy Equipment Staging Area.

On 13 June 1972, thirty-three aircraft of Attack Carrier Air Wing Three, embarked in USS SARATOGA (CVA-60) conducted a complicated, three-pronged, coordinated strike against a major line of communications segment, deep in North Vietnam around the city of Phu Ly. Primary targets included major north/south railway and highway bridges, a very large transshipment point between the railway, highway, and waterway junction, and a heavy concentration of heavy equipment. Target area dispersion of two and one half miles, further complicated by lack of recent intelligence on anticipated heavy anti-aircraft and SAM defenses presented a significant planning challenge. CDR James H. Flatley III planned, weaponeered, and lead all strike and support elements in a precisely and extremely accurate weapons delivery by every strike element. WALLEYE elements, in initiating the attack, scored two direct hits on the railway bridge, while absorbing intense AAA and automatic weapons fire. All remaining strike elements blanketed their respective targets in perfect unison, mutually absorbing the sustained AAA while individually avoiding six surface-to-air missiles fired during the course of the strike. The excellent integrity maintained by the egressing strike elements was further enhanced by the professional airmanship of the Iron Hand leader who effectively suppressed defenses thoughout the duration of the strike and subsequently exposed himself to the concentrated efforts of ground defenses while successfully extricating his disoriented wingman from the target area. Employment of Standard Arm also lent to the successful return of all aircraft. Immediate post strike photography taken by the photo-reconnaissance aircraft, following a long and strongly opposed profile through an area of known intensive defense, revealed all targets completely blanketed. This was substantiated by Strike Leader hand held BDA photography. Subsequent BDA photography revealed one span of the railway bridge down and the abutment to another span heavily damaged, the narrow strand supporting the highway bridge was rendered impassable due to heavy cratering and undermining, the large transshipment point and storage area was 75% destroyed, and the heavy equipment concentration severely damaged. MIGCAP elements holding highly exposed areas supported the strike group most effectively, particularly during the egress of Iron Hand and TARCAP elements. The flawless executon of the strike, despite geographic complexity, target area dispersion, and intensive enemy defense, inflicted extensive and lasting damage on the enemy's capability to support its Southern Offensive.

An F-4B of VF-114 with a full air-to-air load of four Sparrows and four Sidewinders, flies over the Gulf of Tonkin during March of 1968. The open door on the fuselage side is the auxiliary engine bay cooling door. (U.S. Navy)

As an indication of the hazards faced and the results gained from this mission, forty-four decorations for aircrews were recommended. This mission is also noteworthy because SARATOGA had only been on the line for ten days of its first Vietnam combat cruise when it was flown. As an East Coast carrier, SARATOGA and Air Wing Three had not expected to go to WESTPAC. In fact, they were preparing for a Med cruise when the North Vietnamese 1972 Easter Offensive escalated the war. Emergency orders were issued changing SARATOGA's schedule and ordering her to get underway immediately for WESTPAC. All leaves were canceled and some seventy-five personnel were recalled from distant leaves. Thirteen new aircrewmen were welcomed to VF-31, as well as a new "gunner" and his chief. Training during the twenty-eight day transit was intensive. As a result, fifteen of the sixteen aircrew teams, who flew together for the first time only four days prior to commencing combat operations, had no coordination problems in the combat that followed.

On 4 July 1972 the North Vietnamese broadcast the following account of the air war:

Bright stars in the sky. When Nguyen V. and his men came back from a meeting, it was very late and the waning moon was hanging just overhead. He lay wide-awake for a long time, thinking of his comrades, who were all very young and recalling the exploits his unit had made in the six years of its existence. In the latest combat, his unit had shattered an A-6 over Thanh Hoa Province. It was the 99th US aircraft his unit had been credited with having shot down and the pilot was captured.

In another dog fight over Hanoi, young Ngo G had shot down COL Norman Gaddis, who used to train pilots for F-4s. Nguyen P, another young pilot, who was seeing action for the first time, shattered an A-4 and the American pilot, who had logged over 3,000 hours, was taken prisoner...and this despite the fact that our pilots most of the time had to cope with an enemy from four to eight and even twenty times numerically superior. Many combats were given by a single flight of our aircraft which, nevertheless, could hold out against 30 to 40 enemy planes and even succeeded in knocking down two or three of them, or more.

Tonight, Nguyen V., like all his comrades, was thinking of the future combat which would enable his unit to bag the 100th US aircraft to mark the 82nd birth anniversary of President Ho Chi Mihn.

The following day he was ready at his post together with the men of his unit. Noon was setting in. The heat was unbearable. There was not the slightest wind. Our pilots, in their flight suits, waited in the cockpits of their machines.

Then word came for the takeoff. Four MiGs taxied out of their hangar, turned onto the runway and soon disappeared in the horizon, leaving behind long trails of smoke.

They spotted the enemy at area H. The Air Pirates, who an hour ago had sustained stunning defeats in the sky over Hanoi and Haiphong, were very cautious. Nguyen V., at the head of his comrades, pounced on the US planes, which were fanning out in combat formation. Our MiGs, gaining vantage points, closed in upon them while trying to dodge their fire. At the third minute, Nguyen V, who was giving chase to an F-4, realized that he was dogged by another. He ordered numbers 3 and 4 to take care of the first enemy plane and sidetracked his pursuer. The enemy, losing his prey, was visibly perplexed. Then, a missile was fired point-blank at him, making him burn and swirl toward the ground.

It was 1:59 PM on 10 May 1972 and the enemy plane was recorded as the 100th knocked down by the unit. On the way back, Nguyen V. and his men made a tour of Hanoi. Over the Ba Dihn Square, they dipped their wings to salute the late President, of venerated memory.

The North Vietnamese account of the activities of 10 May 1972 does not record the fact that this was the single biggest MiG-killing day of the war for US fighters. On that day, eleven of Nguyen's buddies failed to come home.

In the nine months of this cruise, VF-31 flew 3,365 day hours and 1,077 night hours (of which 4,216 were combat hours). The squadron flew 2,165 sorties, made 1,687 day traps, 536 night traps (167 were Mode ACLS Automatic Carrier Landing System landings, the system Flatley had worked on at Pax River), and 1,639 tons of ordnance were delivered. The only MiG engagement resulted in the shootdown of a MiG-21 by the squadron XO, CDR Sam Flynn. Although many MiG vectors were flown, the MiG controllers managed to keep the enemy fighters away from CVW-3 aircraft. Aircraft utilization was as high as 97 percent on some of the line periods, an amazing figure, considering the maintenance intensive nature of the Phantom. The only squadron aircraft unable to return to the ship because of combat damage made a successful landing at Danang in minimum weather conditions. There were no combat losses of aircraft or personnel on this cruise, an impressive testament to Jim Flatley's leadership.

An impressive testament to Flatley's humor is the speech given to members of Fighter Wing One, the Oceana-based East Coast fighter

An F-4B of VF-114 crosses the ramp just prior to touch down aboard USS KITTY HAWK during February of 1969. The Phantom has an unusual configuration of three fuel tanks, Sidewinders on the inboard pylon missile rails, and TERS on the lower portion of the inboard plyons. (U.S. Navy)

An F-4J of the Operational Test and Evaluation Force squadron, VX-4, vents fuel as it makes a touch and go landing. It is armed with a shark-mouthed 20MM gun pod on the centerline station.

VX-5 did airborne testing of various armament and electronic systems with this F4H-1 (F-4A), the fifth Phantom off the McDonnell production line. (McDonnell Aircraft)

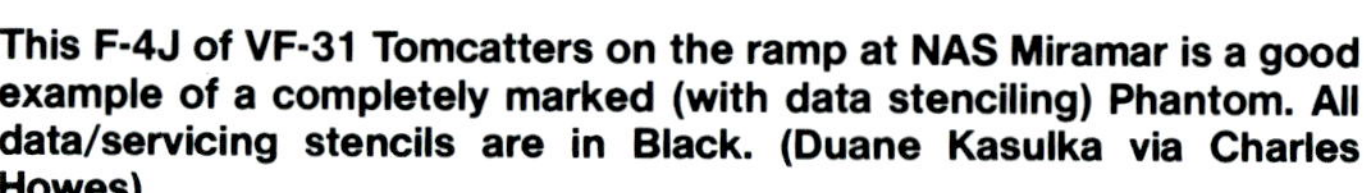

This F-4J of VF-31 Tomcatters on the ramp at NAS Miramar is a good example of a completely marked (with data stenciling) Phantom. All data/servicing stencils are in Black. (Duane Kasulka via Charles Howes)

The VF-114 CAG Phantom spotted on the port deck edge of USS KITTY HAWK (CVA-63) during 1972. All VF-114 aircraft carried the Orange fuselage stripe, fin cap, and Orange BC comic strip Aardvark on the tail. (Nicholas J. Waters III)

The Aardvark of VF-114 donned a special multi-colored scarf and a leather flying helmet when carried on NH 200, the squadron's CAG Phantom. (Nicholas J. Waters III)

community. The subject of the speech was the shut down of the Hot Pad at NAS Key West, Florida. Units from FitWing One had manned the Hot Pad since the Cuban Missile Crisis, standing guard against the threat of communist attack...when they weren't sun-bathing or scuba diving. Although he had his tongue firmly in cheek, there was no doubting the genuine regret expressed by the loss of the plum that was Key West Hot Pad Duty. The Hot Pad shut down had been precipitated by the loss of an F-4, which went into the ocean at the end of the runway. The speech was given under the title:

Fiscal Year 1975 Fighter Fickle Finger of Fate Citation

During a year made noteworthy by office absenteeism and paddleball court diplomacy, one dynamic and far-reaching (although, in truth, not completely altruistically motivated) decision emerged from the hallowed halls at the southern end of Hangar 500. After many years of attempting, unsuccessfully, to support the community's secondary mission of providing operationally ready fighter forces to our carriers in the Mediterranean, the fighter wing decided to take a different tack.

Carefully analyzing the community's low manning level, lack of supervisory personnel, and a nearly destitute material posture, the staff concentrated on devising a better method of improving upon the community's primary mission, and thereby provide a more favorable meterological atmosphere in which staff members could, at discrete intervals, bask themselves in sabbatical splendor. Thus the fighter wing aggressively fostered and brought to fruition the now infamous concept of air wing CONUS-based F-4 Detachments, whose sole purpose would be to fulfill the community's primary mission of manning the Key West Hot Pad.

For those who may not know, the Key West Hot Pad was for fourteen years Naval Aviation's contribution to the nation's southern defense. In fact, in an organization in which the average life of a specific plan of action is only a few hours, Hot Pad stood out for years as the one single stable factor in a squadron's shore-based training cycle. Come hell or high water, Hot Pad was always there. Many of us in attendance this evening have fond memories of duty with the fabled Detachment 14. It offered good flying, fishing, skin diving, quiet tropical evenings at Fort Taylor's "O" Club, the Inner Circle, Big Daddy's or the Boca Chica Bar; a welcome respite to Oceana's drab and drizzily winters or hot and muggy summers.

So into this tropical paradise, who should appear but a key member of the Fighter Wing Staff in the guise of senior officer present. Within hours, the tradition of calm, competent and professional performance of duty was scuttled in favor of a highly sophisticated brand of buck-passing and decision avoidance. Decisive decision-making and dedication to mission accomplishment became a thing of the past. Instead, missions of a higher priority came to the forefront. Missions such as:

F-4 salt water bouyancy tests
Simulated combat attrition effects on sortie rates
Cross country instrument and navigation training
Communications exercises to test facilities at the BOQ Bar and NAS Tennis Courts.

(Above) While he was Commander of the Air Group (CAG) aboard USS INDEPENDENCE during 1975, then CAPT Flatley made a record setting 1,419th 'trap' (arrested landing) flying a VF-102 F-4S Phantom. (U.S. Navy)

CAPT James Flatley and son in the cockpit of an F-4B of VF-31 aboard USS SARATOGA prior to one of Jim Flatley's many record-setting arrested landings. (Robert L. Lawson via RADM James Flatley)

(Below) An F-4S Phantom of VF-31 the 'Felix the Cat' squadron, flown by CAPT Flatley is directed to the catapult aboard USS SARATOGA. The F-4S was a modernized and rebuilt F-4J. (Robert L.Lawson via RADM James H. Flatley III)

An F-4S of VF-31 just milliseconds away from a perfect three wire trap aboard USS SARATOGA. All pilots tried to catch the number three arresting wire, which was considered by the LSO to be a perfect landing. (Tailhook Photo Service)

Well, in a matter of days, CINCLANTFLT, who had been initially impressed with the dynamic new situation in Key West, came to the conclusion that the Hot Pad DET was more of a threat to our national survival than were our southern enemies. Detachment 14 was summarily disestablished. Unfortunately, the actual accomplishment of the dissolution of Hot Pad was delayed several days because the Fighter Wing Senior Officer Present was skin diving on Sugar Loaf Key with his wife and kids, and couldn't be reached. DET personnel reacted brilliantly without leadership, however, and evacuated Key West, less one F-4 aquarium display that will forever sit, partially submerged, as a monument: the visible portion to the many professionals who manned Hot Pad so gloriously for fourteen years, mishap-free; the submerged portion...well, that's better left to everyone's imagination.

For this unparalelled effrontery to common sense, for destroying fourteen years of beautiful tradition, and somehow, at the same time, still sticking the fleet with the CONUS-based detachments, it is indeed a pleasure for the fleet units to present the Fighter Fickle Finger of Fate Award for 1975 to none other than our own Fighter Wing One Staff.

Phantoms of VF-32 (upper) and VF-102 (lower) fly formation with a flight of A-7Bs from VA-82 enroute to targets in North Vietnam during an Alpha Strike. The strike group was from Air Wing Six aboard USS AMERICA (CVA-66). (U.S. Navy)

Yellow Shirts walk alongside NH203, an F-4J of VF-114 aboard USS KITTY HAWK (CV-63). The Yellow Shirts directed the tractor driver and made sure the wings and tail cleared other aircraft.

BILL "BURNER" BEARDSLEY

Bill "Burner" Beardsley flew the F-4 in two of the most demanding missions imaginable. Flying combat missions from a carrier is about as adrenaline-pumping a mission as there is, but a close second would be a half hour or more mission with your canopy three feet from the lead aircraft's wingtip. Burner flew Phantoms with the Blue Angels after he completed his combat tour.

Bill Beardsley joined the Navy in 1965 and earned his Wings of Gold during 1966. He went straight to the Phantom, joining VF-102 as a very junior Ensign "Nugget" (he was the junior officer in the Air Wing). It was during this time that he acquired the nickname "Burner" which has stuck to this day. In fact, he says;

Even my Dad calls me Burner. The handle, unfortunately, did not refer to any wild lifestyle. As a young fighter pilot, I had my share of difficulty in join-ups, maintaining position, and I was liberal in my use of afterburner. I was always the first guy on the tanker and spent more time on the tanker than everyone else. In the years that followed, I became much more judicious in my fuel use, but the name has stuck.

During 1968, VF-102 was based at NAS Oceana, Virginia and was flying off of USS AMERICA (CVA-66).

We went to Vietnam during 1968. The tour lasted about a year, counting the transit times, with actual line periods (combat) of about six months. This was after the post-Tet bombing restriction on North Vietnam above the 19th parallel had gone into effect, so we really didn't have any of the large 'Alpha' strikes going into North Vietnam. As a consequence, we also did not encounter the high levels of SAM and MiG activity that were associated with strikes around the Hanoi-Haiphong areas. Most of our targets were storage areas, water-borne shipping, or just about anything we could find that was enroute to the south. We also flew a lot of night missions attempting to interdict weapons and supplies for the NVA in the south.

Night missions are exciting. Typically you would go off in pairs and you would have to coordinate with the other squadrons to make sure that you weren't all over the same area at the same time. That worked most of the time, but the scariest thing that happened to me during that whole cruise was coming within about a half a second of hitting another F-4, which was on a 90 degree crossing course at my altitude. It was a moonless night and we always turned off all of our lights as soon as we crossed the coast, so it was tough to spot another aircraft unless he was real close. The usual flight makeup was a pair of F-4s, with an A-6 in the lead to find targets with his sophisticated radar. We would try to stagger our ingress times throughout the night. Night missions would start about 2200 (10 PM) and run until 1000 (10 AM) the next day. Usually there would be about eight launches and recoveries of aircraft, so you had flight deck operations going on all night long. Most of these missions were against pre-briefed targets, although bridges were always considered targets of opportunity and, since the North Vietnamese were adept at building bridges overnight, we were always on the lookout for them at logistic chokepoints. We were also tasked with flying Combat Air Patrol all night long. This was MIGCAP over the carrier, or BARCAP in close to the beach.

I don't recall ever having any MiG activity at night, although we did have two or three MiG engagements during the day, and our sister squadron did shoot down a MiG during this cruise, (On 10 July 1968, LT Roy Cash, Jr. and LT Joseph E. Cain, Jr. of VF-33 got a MiG-21 with a Sidewinder) and my Commanding Officer was shot down by a MiG. The MiGs would usually launch from the Hanoi area, feint towards the south...which caused us to launch all of our MIGCAP fighters...then turn around and head back to Hanoi. It was rare for them to continue on south and actually engage us. (From May until September of 1968, seven MiGs were shot down and six of the seven were bagged in the area just south of the 19th parallel. The seventh was a little further south.) The North Vietnamese had a pretty sophisticated ground-controlled-intercept (CGI) network and were also good at jamming radio transmissions. In the case of my skipper's shoot-down, his wingman saw the MiG behind him and was calling for him to break, but his radios were jammed, and the skipper didn't hear the warning.

All of our missions were north of the DMZ, so we tried to stay above 3,500 feet to avoid small-arms fire. We lost two other aircraft to ground fire, one to a SAM and the other to AAA. One of

Burner Beardsley pauses during preflight inspection of the bomb load on his Phantom. The F-4 is armed with Cluster Bomb Units (CBUs) and a 20MM Vulcan gun pod on the centerline station. The gun pod was rarely carried by Navy Phantoms. (Burner Beardsley)

Burner Beardsley and his Radar Intercept Officer (RIO) Mike Joslin board their F-4 on the deck of USS AMERICA during 1968. The mirrors mounted inside the canopy railings helped the pilot and RIO watch the Phantom's 'six' for any attacking MiGs. (U.S. Navy)

Burner had the inscription *TO HO FROM SUSAN* chalked onto a Mk 82 500 pound bomb, which he later dropped over North Vietnam. Susan was a girlfriend of Burner's during 1968. (Burner Beardsley)

those was the escort of the RA-5C Vigilante photo reconnaissance aircraft. The "Vigi's" only defense was speed, so they would normally accelerate to about Mach 1.5 or so before coasting in to take their pictures. Most of our intelligence came from those pictures, since we had no FAC to work with, so the "Vigi" was always escorted.

In all of that time, I never had what I would consider a 'most memorable' mission. I flew 126 combat missions, about half and half bombing or MIGCAP. After the first few times over the beach...looking down and realizing that this was hostile country and those muzzle flashes were guns being shot at you by people who wanted to kill you...once the novelty of that feeling wore off, it became sort of routine, if you didn't get hit...and I never did.

After we left Vietnam, there were a few other short deployments before I was reassigned as an instructor pilot at NAS Miramar. I applied for and was accepted to the Blue Angels, joining the team during 1970. When you join the Blues, it's like learning to fly all over again...it is just a completely different environment. There is nothing comparable to it in fleet operations.

The VF-102 ready room, as seen by Burner Beardsley. He remarked; "They all think I'm number one!" Middle front is Chuck Parish...later shot down and KIA. His father-in-law was Admiral (later FAA Chief) Don Engen. (Burner Beardsley)

VF-102 aviators (left to right) LT Mike Joslin, LT Bill Beardsley, LCDR Peter B. Booth and his RIO. LT Joslin was later killed in a crash while LCDR Booth later retired from the Navy after attaining the rank of Rear Admiral. (Burner Beardsley)

I can't compare the Phantom to any other team aircraft, because the F-4 was the only aircraft the team had during my tour. I flew the F-11 Tiger during flight training, which was the predecessor to the Phantom, and it was a real solid formation aircraft. The F-4, on the other hand, has a lot of wing vortices...a lot of push-pull...when you get that close, but that is something that you get used to. During my tour I flew number Three...left wing...in the diamond. My impression of the F-4 in that mission is that it was a big, physical aircraft, and it took a strong physical person to fly it properly. Its brute size and the noise it made gave it a presence some of the other team aircraft have not had. But it was expensive to operate and hard to maintain in terms of the number of people required to keep all the systems running. The accident rate was high too, although there didn't seem to be any single common thread running through the accidents the Blues had with the Phantom. I think we used up fourteen or fifteen aircraft in the time period that the Blues had the Phantom.

One of the things that made the Blues Phantoms different was the trim system we had installed in our aircraft. We had a series of springs, levers, and cams back in the tail section which gave us thirty pounds of stick pull with full nose-down trim, which is what we flew the shows with. That meant that no matter what the stick position was (forward or aft), it took thirty pounds of pressure to move it. In most aircraft, the controls tend to get "soft" as you go slower, but with this set up we maintained a constant thirty pounds of required pull to move the stick. The Air Force was flying the F-4E during the same time that we were flying the F-4J. They had a bellows unit in the tail which programmed more pull on the stick as you went faster. So for any given trim position, the higher the speed, the more pull you had. I believe this was a better system.

One of the typical air show maneuvers is a loop, which we would start at 450 knots, with the stick relatively far forward. Going over the top of the loop, inverted, we might be down to 130 knots, with the stick all the way back in our laps. That was a significant amount of stick movement, all with thirty pounds of pull, so if you are not a real physical person, it can be real tough. And I was not a real physical person, so I did have a tough time. In fact, during my first practice sessions, I could only do a couple of maneuvers, then would have to pull out of the formation to rest my arm. The philosophy behind this control arrangement had to do with prevention of pilot-induced oscillations (PIO). The Blues F-4 diamond formation had the leader's wingtip over

A deck crewman jockies an auxiliary power cart into position to start an F-4J of VF-92 aboard USS CONSTELLATION during September of 1974. The Red intake covers on the Phantom prevented foreign objects from being injested into the engines during start-up. (U.S. Navy)

Red shirts (ordnancemen) load an AIM-7 Sparrow missile into the rear missile well of an F-4J of VF-96 aboard USS CONSTELLATION on 1 May 1972. The second Sparrow, on the missile cart, will be loaded into the forward missile well. (U.S. Navy)

the top of the wingmans rear canopy, with about two to three feet of separation. When you are that close, you can run into the other aircraft in a split second, with only the slightest control input.

In a "trimmed out" configuration, you could get into a PIO real easy, as you chased the proper position through the neutral stability regime. We cranked out the rudder pedals almost all the way out, so that our knees were raised, giving us an arm/wrist rest. Then, with that constant thirty pounds of pull, you were less likely to overcontrol the aircraft. The lead and solo aircraft did not have to fly this way, although I think Harley Hall did. (Hall was team leader in 1971 and was the last American pilot shot down in the Vietnam War.) The rest of us had to learn at what point during the show that we could run some of that tremendous trim pressure out and relax our arm muscles, because no matter how strong you were, you could put your arm to sleep with a half an hour of that kind of pressure. We would usually climb out of the aircraft soaking wet from the physical and mental grunting and grinding during a show.

Burner left the Navy after his tour with the Blues and went to work for Delta Airlines, guaranteeing himself a flying future. He has not lost his love of aerobatics and has owned both a Pitts S-2 and Citabria.

An F-4J of VF-92 high over the Gulf of Tonkin on 4 May 1972. The Phantom is configured with missiles and three fuel tanks. This configuration was used for extended Combat Air Patrol (CAP) missions. (U.S. Navy)

A grinning LT Bill 'Burner' Beardsley, the Number Three Blue Angel poses in the cockpit of his Blue Angels F-4J Phantom II. (U.S. Navy)

(Above) An F-4J of VF-92 launches from the waist catapult of USS CONSTELLATION (CVA-64). The large trailing edge flaps and 'drooped' leading edge slats help increase lift at this critical stage of flight. (Tailhook Photo Service)

(Above) LT Jay Tinker preflights his F-4J of VF-92 prior to an air strike over South Vietnam on 1 May 1972. The TER (Triple Ejector Rack) on the inboard pylon carries a full load of three Mk-82 low drag 500 pound bombs. (U.S. Navy)

(Below) The turret man of an MB-5 crash truck stands by, ready to render assistance should this F-4J of VF-92 landing aboard CONSTELLATION on 24 January 1972 run into trouble. (U.S. Navy)

(Below) A pilot's eye view of the entrance to the main channel of Haiphong harbor, North Vietnam. Hiaphong Harbor was one of the most heavily defended areas in all of North Vietnam. (U.S. Navy)

(Above) An F-4J of VF-213 Black Lions is refueled by a KA-6D of VA-52 Knightriders. Both squadrons were part of Carrier Air Wing 11 aboard USS KITTY HAWK engaged in operations against North Vietnam during 1972. (Nicholas J. Waters III)

(Below) An F-4J of VF-114 taxies to the forward catapult aboard KITTY HAWK during flight operations on Yankee Station during the Summer of 1972. The fuselage stripe and fin cap were Orange as was the 'BC' comic strip Aardvark on the tail. (Nicholas J. Waters III)

(Above) An F-4J of VF-213 is moved past other Black Lions' Phantoms and an F-4J of VF-114 on the deck of USS KITTY HAWK (CVA-63) while operating on Yankee Station during 1972. (Nicholas J. Waters III)

An F-4J Phantom of VF-114 goes off the angle deck of USS KITTY HAWK, while a pair of A-6 Intruders are moved into postion for launch off the bow catapults during operations in the Gulf of Tonkin in the Summer of 1972.

(Above) Deck crewmen rest during a break in cyclic flight ops aboard the USS CORAL SEA (CVA-43). With a twelve hour per day flight schedule, deck crews relaxed whenever the opportunity presented itself. (U.S. Navy)

(Above) An F-4J Phantom of VF-213 high over North Vietnam while on a MIGCAP mission during 1972. NH-113 has both auxiliary engine bay air cooling doors on the fuselage sides open. (Nicholas J. Waters III)

(Below) This VF-114 Phantom sports a small North Vietnamese flag MiG kill marking on the splitter plate. VF-114 scored five kills during the war; two MiG-17s, two MiG-21s, and an AN-2 Colt biplane transport. (Nicholas J. Waters III)

(Below) Shooting flames from both afterburners, an F-4J of VF-213 runs up to full power just prior to launch from the outboard waist catapult aboard USS KITTY HAWK during 1972. (Nicholas J. Waters III)

(Below) This F-4J of VF-114 aboard USS KITTY HAWK (CV-63) was flown by the squadron commanding officer and carried the name *SKIPPER SMITH* on the fuselage side in Orange, outlined in Black. (Nicholas J. Waters III)

(Below) An F-4J of VF-114 Aardvarks taxies forward aboard USS KITTY HAWK during 1972. The Aardvarks and Air Group 11 were teamed with CVA-63 from 1962 through the entire life of the squadron's Phantom experience. (Nicholas J. Waters III)

TUCKER'S MiG KILL - 10 AUGUST 1972

I was deployed to the Western Pacific as Operations Officer of the "Sluggers", Fighter Squadron 103 (VF-103), commanded by CDR Bob Cowles. We were part of Carrier Air Wing Three (CVW-3), commanded by one of the top tacticians of that time, CDR "Deke" Bordone. We were operating from USS SARATOGA (CVA-60) commanded by then CAPT 'Sandy' Sanderson and the embarked Carrier Group Commander was RADM Jack Christianson.

The two fighter squadrons on SARATOGA each maintained a continuous "Alert Five" F-4J Phantom crew on the flight deck during periods specified by CTF-77. This duty rotated among the carriers on Yankee Station, usually in twelve to twenty-four hour increments.

On 10 August 1972, from 1800-2000 my RIO, LTJG Bruce Edens and I were standing the "Alert Five" for VF-103. Ironically, it was not our turn, but we had agreed to trade places with our squadron Executive Officer, CDR Danny Michaels, who had to attend a meeting. Another crew from our sister squadron, VF-31 "Tomcatters" was also standing the watch.

The first indication that anything was happening was a loud "Launch the Alert Five" over the 5MC (flight deck PA system) and 1MC (ships PA system) at just about sunset. I was sitting on the starter tractor, drafting proposed changes to the squadron's Standard Operating Procedures. Bruce was in the back seat, strapped in, as we were supposed to be. He started yelling at me to get in and get the bird started. Ever since early in my first Phantom squadron tour, I have done a "scramble" start each and every start, so I was well prepared for the simultaneous strap in and fast start I had to do right then. I was quickly ready to taxi from my spot just aft of the island to the catapult. Because of the requirement to be able to launch the Alert Five fighters immediately from any catapult, in any sea state or natural wind condition, we were not loaded with a full bag of fuel. As I was spotted on the catapult, I was ordered to take on a full bag of fuel, since there was no longer an active contact and the ship was making plenty of wind to launch me. I didn't know it at the time, but later found out that the MiG, which had been tracked from the vicinity of Kep on a southerly track, had disappeared from the scopes in the vicinity of Vinh.

We were loaded with two AIM-7E Sparrows on the aft fuselage stations, two AIM-9D Sidewinders on the wing stations, a centerline fuel tank, and empty TERs on the outboard wing stations (the F-4s had been doing a lot of bombing and we frequently left the airplane configured for bombing missions with TERs on the wing stations.)

As I completed fueling, the MiG reappeared in the vicinity of Vinh, and I was given a vector and launched. I stayed right on the deck as I made a hard starboard turn off the cat to a westerly heading, accelerating in afterburner to 450 knots before starting to climb. I had launched shortly after sunset. I was given a couple of bogie calls...he was west of me at some 70 miles...and then he disappeared from the controllers scope again. Bruce and I were disappointed as we were told to max endure and take up a CAP station at 15,000 feet in the vicinity of Hon Mat Island just off the Son Ca river mouth east of Vinh. The VF-31 F-4 launched shortly after we did, followed by a VA-75 KA-6D tanker. The tanker reached our vicinity and Bruce and I joined him and commenced topping off...just in case. It was completely dark by now. We were almost completed tanking when our controller asked which F-4 was on the tanker. I suspected his reason for asking was that the bogey contact had reappeared and I was just about to tell Bruce not to say anything. I unplugged, but before I could warn Bruce, he had acknowledged that we were on the tanker. Sure enough, the controller had the bogey contact and they quickly vectored the VF-31 Phantom for him. The MiG was about 10 to 12 miles west of us. The controller advised the VF-31 Phantom driver not to go feet dry without a radar contact on the bogey.

LTJG Bruce Edens and LCDR Gene Tucker pose with their freshly painted MiG kill marking shortly after their 10 August 1972 MiG kill. The MiG kill marking is a Red star, with a Black MiG-21 and a White Sparrow missile. (U.S. Navy via Gene Tucker)

I immediately turned west, estimating that I was about five miles north of the other Phantom and five miles off the coast. The VF-31 Phantom called no contact and that he was turning right to parallel the coast. I called him and asked him to turn left, away from me, so that he wouldn't interfere with my search. I then asked the controller for "bogey dope". We were told he was at 8,000 feet, 140 degrees at twelve miles from us. I descended quickly to 8,000 feet and Bruce got a radar contact southwest at twelve miles almost immediately. The bogey was tracking north and we rolled in about eight miles behind him. I lit the afterburner, accelerated to about 650 knots, and closed to about four to five miles...that's when we lost radar contact. We were closing rather rapidly and I didn't want to overrun him, so I slowed to about 400 knots while doing a left 90 degree turn, then back immediately to the northerly heading. We realized that he had probably descended, so I let down immediately to 3,500 feet. On my previous combat cruise, we had operated extensively in this area, and I knew that the highest karst was 3,500 feet, so I wasn't concerned about running into a mountain. As soon as we reached 3,500 feet, Bruce reacquired the bogey about six to seven miles in front of us. I remember saying to myself; "Tucker, this is probably your last chance to get this guy, or any other MiG, so you'd better make it quick and good." As soon as Bruce got the radar contact, I re-lit the afterburners and accelerated to 650 knots. As I was approaching 650 knots, it occurred to me that I should jettison the centerline tank and the TERs. My airspeed was well above the published jettison limits, but I applied about two positive G and jettisoned the partially full centerline tank. The was a mild "thump" as it cleanly departed the airplane (due to the speed, there was already a mild buffet). Then I jettisoned the TERs, putting 1.5G or less on the airplane. There was a very pronounced "BANG" as they came off, which really surprised me...which I guess it shouldn't have, since the TERs were far enough out on the wings to develop some pretty good force because of the long moment arm, even though they were light. Now with a clean F-4, I was moving along approaching 750 knots, closing the MiG at something like 300 knots from dir ectly astern.

We closed to about three miles and were inside max range for our Sparrows. Bruce hollered; "SHOOT SHOOT!" But since the MiG was steady in his retreat, I thought we should sweeten it up a bit by closing a little more. I said; "Wait, Wait", and we

An F-4J Phantom of VF-103 takes on fuel from the Buddy store refueling pod carried on an A-7E Corsair II of VA-105. A-7s with Buddy stores augmented other carrier tanker assets (KA-6Ds and KA-3Bs) during high tempo operations. (U.S. Navy via Gene Tucker)

closed to almost two miles before I squeezed off two Sparrows at five second intervals, calling "Fox One" as I fired. The rocket motor was so bright at night that it virtually blinded me for a second. The second Sparrow launched just as the first warhead detonated directly in front of us. There was a large fireball, and the second missile impacted in the same spot. I came right slightly to avoid any debris. The target on our radar appeared to stop in mid-air and within a second or two the radar broke lock. The MiG-21 pilot did not survive. If he ejected after the first missile, the second missile must have done him in. We couldn't see any debris in the dark.

I was pretty upset to hear the controller start calling range and bearing on the bogey after we reported lost contact after splashing him. Because of the distance from us to the controlling ship (100 miles or more), and our relatively low altitude, he did not hear our "Fox One" calls and didn't realize that we had fired. Bruce searched for bogeys with our radar, but we didn't spot anything. This went on for a minute or so, until I realized that the automatic tracking feature of the controllers radar had probably continued plotting the bogeys symbol on the last known course and speed when radar contact was lost. Once we realized we were tracking a phantom bogey, we turned east and coasted out. We were in a fairly hot area...lots of surface-to-air missile and AAA sites, just southwest of Thanh Hoa. We coasted out with lots of fuel (about 9,000 pounds) and returned to the ship for the ever exciting night carrier landing. The kill was confirmed about three days later. The F-4J we were flying, BuNo 157229 VF-103 side number 206, was lost during 1976 as the result of an airborne fire in the Roosevelt Roads operating area, however, the pilot and RIO ejected safely.

We were extremely well prepared for that engagement. When I first went through the F-4 Replacement Air Group, heavy emphasis was placed on instrument flying and pilot capability to complete intercepts at all altitudes and under all weather conditions. I had always worked closely with my RIOs, establishing crew coordination, responsibilities, practicing not only the standard intercepts and air-to-ground work that all crews practiced, but I frequently conducted an intercept to keep my hand in. Occasionally I would close my eyes and have the RIO call my

This VF-103 Phantom was assigned to LCDR Gene Tucker and sported his MiG kill marking, although it was not the F-4J in which he and Bruce Edens actually scored their kill. The kill was made in BuNo 157299, side number AC 206, call sign 'Clubleaf 206'. (Tailhook Photo Service)

'Alert Five' crews normally stood watch strapped into their Phantoms, ready to launch as soon as the word was given and the carrier was turned into the wind. (Jim Hurley)

(Above) A flight of Phantoms from VF-151 return to USS MIDWAY after a 1973 strike against the communist Pathet Lao who, like their North Vietnamese mentors, never recognized the peace treaty. (U.S. Navy)

maneuvers to recover the airplane from an unusual attitude, then call my turns and altitude changes to simulate flying us to a safe area for ejection if I was ever blinded. And Bruce Edens was a top-notch RIO...a knowledgeable Radar Intercept Officer.

In general, I believe we had a distinct advantage over the North Vietnamese, when considering just the airplane and aircrew against each other, not counting the distance from home, SAMs, and AAA. The proven capability of the Sparrow III missile in the forward hemisphere had to be a big psychological factor, even if you grant the fact that the overall probability of kill (PK) of the missile in those days wasn't as good as we would have liked. To see a missile coming at you head-on, or knowing that the F-4 coming at you could fire one, must surely have caused some trepidation in the MiG cockpit.

In the area of aircrew training and experience I feel we had a distinct advantage. We had much more flight time in training and flew an average of twenty-five to forty hours a month consistently. Their flight hours were significantly lower. We were taught the basics, but given the opportunity to think for ourselves in various scenarios. Their flight training and close control intercept techniques were much more restrictive. I also believe our air discipline and section integrity was much better.

There is no arguing that the MiG-17 and MiG-21 were much more maneuverable and could turn better than the F-4. The F-4 had an extremely difficult time turning and could easily decelerate to a point where it was virtually out of energy in a tight turning engagement against a proficient MiG pilot. Unfortunately, it was not until around 1968 that we realized we were seriously deficient in our Air Combat Maneuvering training of Navy pilots and established the Navy Fighter Weapons School (Top Gun) at NAS Miramar. That program was, and continues to be, the finest ACM training in the world.

We also had a distinct advantage in terms of weapons systems. Our radar (pulse or pulse doppler) could detect and track MiG series aircraft at ranges significantly longer than our missiles could shoot, and although our Sparrows and Sidewinders in the period 1965 to 1972 were not as good as they are today, they were certainly better than any capability the MiGs had. The only sour note is that the lack of a gun on the F-4 was a serious design mistake. Fortunately, all fighters designed since the F-4 have included an internal gun.

(Right) An F-4B of VF-161 Chargers aboard USS MIDWAY during the 1972 bombing campaign against North Vietnam. The aircraft's plane captain and squadron engine mechanics are running checks on the starboard engine. (U.S. Navy)

(Below) An F-4J of VF-96 and and RA-5C Vigilante of RVAH-12 are prepared for launch aboard USS CONSTELLATION. The catapult bridle on the Phantom has been checked and the deck crewman is running clear as the Catapult Officer gives the signal to run up the engines to full power. (Tailhook Photo Service)

(Left) A section of F-4Js of VF-92 aboard USS CONSTELLATION fly a Barrier Combat Air Patrol (BARCAP) mission over the northern Gulf of Tonkin. BARCAPS were long boring patrols with little action. (Tailhook Photo Service)

(Below) A section of F-4J Phantoms of VF-96 Fighting Falcons refuel from a Buddy store equipped A-7E Corsair II of VA-146 over the Gulf of Tonkin during 1972. (U.S. Navy)

(Above) This F-4J of VF-96 carries eight small North Vietnamese flag markings for the eight MiG kills credited to the squadron. Additionally, the Phantom carries the ADM Clifton award marking low on both intake splitter plates. This veteran of Southeast Asia was at NAS Glenview, Illinois during 1973. (Charles Howes)

(Right) LT Matt Connelly describes the action to his RIO, LT Tom Blonski, after their double MiG-17 kill of 10 May 1972. VF-96 pilots shot down a total of six MiGs on that day. Connelly's aircraft was F-4J BuNo 155769, call sign 'Showtime 106'. (U.S. Navy)

(Below) This F-4J of VF-96 landing at NAS Atsugi, Japan during 1970, was flown by the CAG aboard USS AMERICA and carries the same markings applied to the triple MiG killer Phantom flown by Randy Cunningham on 10 May 1972. (Shinichi Ohtaki)

(Above) A pristine F-4B Phantom of VF-161 prior to going aboard USS MIDWAY for the summer of 1972 combat cruise. VF-161 used the call sign 'Rock River' which all but replaced the official nickname of Chargers. The Black tail with Red lightning bolt was one of the most striking paint schemes used on the Phantom.

(Left) A pair of RA-5C Vigilantes of RVAH-12 and a pair of F-4J Phantoms of VF-92 impersonate the Blue Angels during a practice formation flight. This flight was not a combat mission! (Tailhook Photo Service)

(Below) An F-4J of VF-21 assigned to the Air Group Commander (CAG) aboard USS RANGER after the squadron returned to its home base of NAS Miramar, Calif. during the fall of 1973. (R.J. Archer)

(Above) Each squadron in the air wing assigns its '00' aircraft to CAG and marks it appropriately. This F-4J is the CAG airplane of VF-154 and it carries a rainbow of squadron colors on the lower rudder.

(Right) This F-4J of VF-31 (BuNo 157308) carried this personal marking on the nose wheel door. Personal markings on Navy aircraft during the Vietnam War were usually confined to the nose wheel door, if allowed at all. (Jim Sullivan)

(Below) A section of F-4Js of VF-154 enroute to a target in Laos on 15 June 1973. The signing of the Paris peace accords meant a return of POWs and a cessation of the bombing of North Vietnam. The North Vietnamese, however, continued operations in Laos and the air war over these countries continued. (U.S. Navy)

(Above) CDR Sam Flynn's MiG-killing F-4J BuNo 157293, of VF-31, call sign 'Bandwagon 101'. Flynn knocked down a MiG-21 Fishbed fighter with an AIM-9 Sidewinder air-to-air missile on 21 June 1972.

(Above) Catapult crewmen direct an F-4B of VF-14 to the number two catapult aboard USS JOHN F KENNEDY during 1969. Depending upon launch weight, the steam catapult could accelerate the Phantom from zero to one hundred and sixty miles an hour in two hundred and fifty feet. (U.S. Navy)

(Above) This VF-111 Sundowners Phantom also has revised markings during February of 1973. The Red and White sunset which once covered the entire tail has been reduced to just the rudder. The only concession to CAG markings is a row of varied colored stars on the fin cap. (Tom Patterson via Norman E. Taylor)

(Below) The catapult officer aboard USS CORAL SEA gives the launch signals to the pilot of this F-4B of VF-51 while operating in the South China Sea during September of 1973. The colorful Screaming Eagle (also known as 'the supersonic can-opener') carried on VF-51 Phantoms during 1972 was replaced by a Black tail. (U.S. Navy)

(Above) Squadron electronic maintenance crewmen work on the pulse doppler air intercept radar of an F-4J of VF-31 on the flight deck of USS SARATOGA (CVA-60) during May of 1969. (U.S. Navy)

(Above) This F-4J of VF-154 off the USS CORAL SEA made it safely back to Danang despite suffering major combat damage over North Vietnam. The Phantom is peppered with numerous holes from a near miss by either a SAM or AAA shell burst.

(Above) An F-4B Phantom of VF-111 Sundowners. VF-111 was credited with two MiG kills during the Vietnam War, one to an F-8 Crusader and one to the F-4 flown by LT Gary Weigand and LTJG Bill Freckelton. (Harry Walker)

(Below) Deck crewmen check the operation of the steam catapult track in preparation for the next cycle of launches of Air Wing Three aircraft aboard USS SARATOGA. (Tailhook Photo Service)

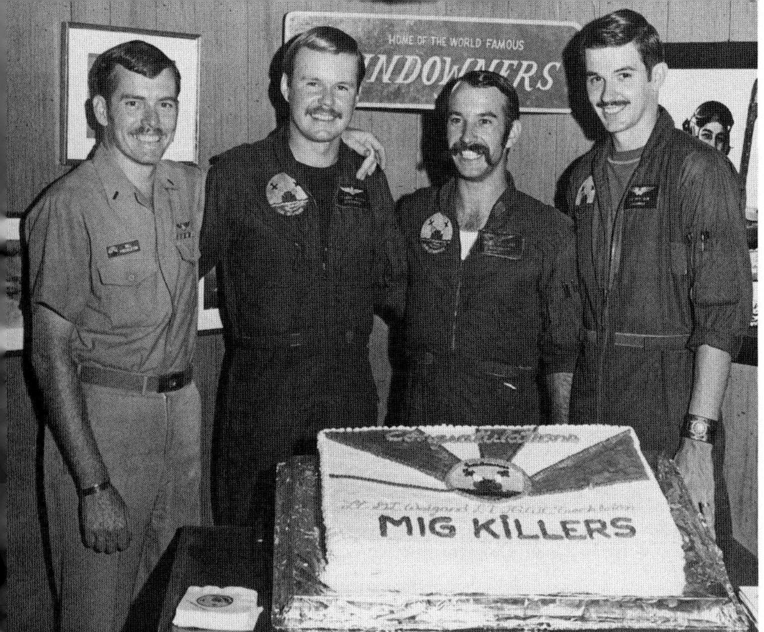

(Above) MiG killers (left to right) LTJG Bill Freckelton and LT Gary Weigand celebrate with the traditional victory cake along with their wingmen in the fight, LT Jim Stillinger and LT Rick Olin. (U.S. Navy)

(Above) Red shirted squadron ordnancemen aboard USS KITTY HAWK roll a bomb cart loaded with three Mk-82 500 pound Snakeye bombs towards a waiting Phantom during 1967. (U.S. Navy)

(Left) The crew of an F-4J Phantom perform preflight equipment checks as they prepare for another mission in the cockpit of their fighter.

LT Paul Bennett of the Royal Navy and CAPT Gene Quist, USAF prepare to launch in a VF-213 F-4J from USS Kitty Hawk in the South China Sea during February of 1976. Now, that's an exchange crew! (U.S. Navy)

LOSSES

The Vietnam War was the longest and most expensive war in American history. Since the Phantom was the most prolific of American fighters involved, it suffered heavy losses. Over twenty-five percent of all Phantoms produced (both domestic and for export) were lost in Southeast Asia! The table below includes both Navy, Marine and USAF losses for the purposes of comparison.

SEA
F-4 LOSSES IN SEA BY TYPE OF LOSS AND YEAR
ALL MODELS
UPDATED: 21 APRIL 1986

			1964	1965	1966	1967	1968	1969	1970	1971	1972	1973	TOTALS	
LOSSES TO MIGS	USAF	F-4			3	9	3			1	17		33	MIGS
		RF-4C											0	
	USN	F-4		1		1	2				1		5	
	USMC	F-4									1		1	
		RF-4B											0	39
LOSSES TO SAMS	USAF	F-4		2	6	3	1			2	16		30	SAMS
		RF-4C				4					3		7	
	USN	F-4		1		5	1			1	5		13	
	USMC	F-4		1									1	
		RF-4B												51
LOSSES TO AAA & SMALL ARMS FIRE	USAF	F-4		10	33	63	50	57	30	22	38	4	307	AAA & SMALL ARMS
		RF-4C			7	16	19	8	9	3	2		64	
	USN	F-4		8	15	17	5	1			5	2	53	
	USMC	F-4		1	10	10	16	13	9	6	65		130	
		RF-4B				1	2						3	557
LOSSES TO ENEMY ATTACKS ON AIR BASES	USAF	F-4				6	3						9	ENEMY ATTACKS ON AIR BASES
		RF-4					4						4	
	USN	F-4											0	
	USMC	F-4					6						6	
		RF-4B											0	19
COMBAT LOSSES	USAF	F-4		12	42	81	57	57	30	25	71	4	379	COMBAT
		RF-4C			7	20	23	8	9	3	6		76	
	USN	F-4		10	15	23	8	1		1	11	2	71	
	USMC	F-4		1	10	10	22	13	9		7		72	
		RF-4B				1	2						3	601
OPERATIONAL LOSSES	USAF	F-4	1	1	14	16	6	7	3	2	11	2	63	OPERA-TIONAL
		RF-4C				3	2	2					7	
	USN	F-4	1	4	3	13	12	5	5	2	5	4	54	
	USMC	F-4		2	2	6	2	5	4		2		23	
		RF-4B				1							1	148
ALL LOSSES TOTALS			1964	1965	1966	1967	1968	1969	1970	1971	1972	1973	TOTAL	
			2	54	167	309	246	177	108	68	266	18	1415	1415

1967 USMC LOSS TO ENEMY ATTACH ON AIR BAGS MAY INCLUDE TWO F-4

Source: Department of Defense.

Some further insight on how the war was fought can be seen in the official listing of aircraft lost to MiGs. Excerpts from that listing showing details of F-4 losses follow:

On 9 April 1965, F-4B BuNo 151403 of VF-96, call sign "Showtime 2", flying from USS RANGER engaged in high altitude aerial combat with four MiG-17s while on a BARCAP mission over water. The Phantom disappeared and was not seen or heard from again. An enemy news release indicated that it had been shot down by the MiGs. Official speculation is that the Phantom pilot tried to turn with the MiGs, got slow, and was shot down by MiG cannon fire.

On 7 December 1965, F-4B BuNo 152261 of VMFA-323 operating out of Danang was on an armed night reconnaissance escort mission when it was hit by an air-to-air missile in Route Package 3.

On 19 November 1967, F-4B BuNo 150997 of VF-151, call sign "Switchbox 110", flying from USS CORAL SEA was jumped by several MiG-17s while on a TARCAP mission in the vicinity of Haiphong. During the fight, the North Vietnamese fired an Atoll AAM which tracked and blew the right wing off the Phantom. The F-4 was at 4,000 feet and 450 knots at the time.

On 19 November 1967, F-4B BuNo 152304 of VF-151, call sign "Switchbox 115" was the wingman of Switchbox 110. The RIO stated that they were hit by either MiG cannon fire or the debris of Switchbox 110 when it blew up. The Phantom went out of control and the crew ejected.

7 May 1968. F-4B BuNo 151485 of VF-92, call sign "Silver Kite 210" off USS ENTERPRISE was engaged with a MiG-17 in the vicinity of Vinh while at Bingo fuel state. Silver Kite 210 was unaware that the MiG was on his tail and shortly after going feet wet at 8,000 feet and 400 Knots, the Phantom was hit by an Atoll AAM. His wingman saw the missile firing hit from seven to eight miles away. Out of control, with all warning lights illuminated, the pilot and RIO ejected.

16 June 1968. F-4J BuNo 155548 of VF-102, call sign "Milkvine 101" operating from USS AMERICA was on MIGCAP mission with a wingman in the vicinity of Vinh Son when they received an

An F-4S of VF-21 is directed into position on the number two cat aboard USS RANGER steaming in the Western Pacific during April of 1976. Once the Phantom is ready for launch the crewman in the foreground will fire the catapult. (U.S. Navy)

The US Seventh Fleet maintained a non-combat presence in the South China Sea after the cut-off of combat funds. This VMFA-115 Phantom is about to launch from USS ENTERPRISE on 15 January 1975. Also on board for that cruise were the first two F-14 Tomcat squadrons, VF-1 and VF-2. (U.S. Navy)

intercept vector from Red Crown (USS CHICAGO). MiGs were sighted at 4 o'clock position and the section broke hard right. The lead MiG-21 fired a heat-seeking missile, which flew up the tailpipe of the lead F-4 and exploded. The crew successfully ejected.

On 27 April 1972, F-4B BuNo 153025 of VF-51, call sign "Screaming Eagle 10" off USS CORAL SEA was jumped by MiGs while on MIGCAP mission near Bai Thuong. The Phantom was hit in starboard engine by an AAM, which resulted in an engine fire and hydraulic failure. The Phantom went out of control and the crew ejected.

On 10 July 1972, F-4J BuNo 155803 of VF-103, call sign "Club Leaf 212", off USS SARATOGA was on MIGCAP in Route Package 6b when jumped by MiG-17s. The Phantom was hit in the aft fuselage by cannon fire, which caused hydraulic and structural failure.

On 26 August 1972, F-4J BuNo 155811 of VMFA-232, call sign "Motion" was on a BARCAP mission out of Nam Phuong, Thailand into Route Package 4 of North Vietnam. The Phantom was jumped by a MiG-21 and hit in tail section by an AAM. The Phantom was seen to explode.

A section of VF-191 F-4Js off the CORAL SEA formate with a KA-6D Intruder of VA-95 during December of 1980. The Satan's Kittens turned in their F-8 Crusaders for the F-4J Phantom after the Vietnam War. (U.S. Navy)

(Above) An unmarked F-4N flies escort on a Soviet Long Range Aviation Tu 95 Bear D reconnaissance aircraft. There are strict international agreements that set the rules governing such escorts both for the Phantom and the Soviet aircraft. (McDonnell Aircraft)

(Right) Another important Navy mission for the Phantom is that of target drone. This bright Red/Orange QF-4 serves as a radio-controlled target at the China Lake Missile Range, however, the aircraft can still be flown by a human crew when necessary. (Shinichi Ohtaki)

(Below) Soviet reconnaissance aircraft routinely overfly American ships. When they are picked up by the carrier's radar, the CAP aircraft are vectored to intercept them before they get to the fleet. This VF-114 F-4S has intercepted a Russian Tu 16 Badger on 9 December 1975 and will escort it until clear of the Battle Group. (U.S. Navy)

(Above) A pair of F-4S Phantoms of VF-301, a Naval Air Reserve squadron, carry the latest three tone Gray Navy tactical camouflage during training exercises on 13 May 1984. (U.S. Navy, PH2 Bruce Trombecky)

(Below) Part of the new tactical camouflage is a false canopy painted under the nose. The false canopy gives the impression that the Phantom is turning into the enemy aircraft when it is actually turning away. (Tailhook Photo Service)

An F-4S of VF-11 out of Naval Air Station Oceana, Virginia is silhouetted against the setting sun as it dumps fuel in preparation for landing. (U.S. Navy)

EPILOG

As far as the United States Navy is concerned the McDonnell-Douglas F-4 Phantom II has passed into Naval Aviation history. On 18 October 1986, a Naval Air Reserve F-4S of VF-202 stationed at NAS Dallas, Texas made the last operational landing by a Phantom on an aircraft carrier, the USS AMERICA. When the squadron returned to Dallas the Phantom was officially retired from the Navy, after twenty-eight years of fleet service. VF-202 would replace their Phantoms with Grumman F-14A Tomcats, while other units have gone on to replace their Phantoms with either Grumman F-14 Tomcats or McDonnell-Douglas F/A-18 Hornets. This next generation of fleet fighters are the high-tech cutting edge of the fleet... fighter/interceptor/attack aircraft that can do everything that the Phantom once did...only far better.

But for a generation of fighter pilots, Radar Intercept Officers (RIOs), maintenancemen, and carrier crewmen... the rallying cry, "Phantoms Phorever" will live in their hearts and minds. For this generation, the big, hulking McDonnell fighter with its upturned wingtips and downturned stabilators will remain a symbol of American technological superiority during a trying time for both the Navy and the nation. The Phantom has come to symbolize the best of Naval Aviation to them and to many of us who never flew, or were associated with the Phantom. If you ever saw one in the air you know that the Phantom was all brute power, noise, smoke, and... presence. If you ever lived near a Naval Air Station, you didn't have to look up to tell when a Phantom was in the landing pattern — its distinctive engine noise identified it, even at night.

Even when the US Air Force, US Marine Corps, and all those foreign air forces (eleven at last count and perhaps more to come) who still fly Phantoms finally retire their F-4s (sometime in the 21st century) it will not be forgotten.

This F-4S of Reserve Squadron VF-202, stationed at NAS Dallas, Texas made the last operational Phantom carrier landing on 18 October 1986 aboard USS AMERICA. VF-202 was the last Navy unit to fly the F-4, later transitioning to the F-14A Tomcat. (U.S. Navy)

Vietnam Studies Group

From Squadron/Signal

6002

6032

6040

6034

6036

6037

6042

6046

6351

squadron/signal publications